W9-BKC-708

This book is a gift to

_____

on the occasion of

_____

Prayers from the Heart

The Sacred Heart University Prayerbook

Edited by

Patricia Leonard Pasley

SACRED HEART UNIVERSITY PRESS
FAIRFIELD, CONNECTICUT

Edited by Patricia Leonard Pasley
Graphic design by Roberta Reynolds

Bless the authors of these prayers.
Bless the hands
that penned each holy word.
Bless the God
who touched the soul
who wrote the prayer
that you now pray,
and every soul who thought to share,
and every word collected here.
May they (and we)
bear a truthful witness
to the God of love
who loves us
enough
to invite us to pray
Amen.

"Prayer consists of attention.
It is the orientation of all the attention
of which the soul is capable towards God."
          -Simone Weil (1909-1943)

The compiling and editing of a prayer book
requires a similar kind of love and attention to detail.
This compilation would not have been possible
were it not for the tireless efforts of

Margaret A. Palliser, OP,

the editor's editor,
who sees what other eyes miss,
who works when others have long gone home,
and whose careful attention to
every detail of this manuscript
has made this book
a thing of beauty
with the power to illuminate the soul.

Preface

I have always been struck by the advice of Father Zossima in Fyodor Dostoyevsky's *The Brothers Karamazov*: "Be not forgetful of prayer. Every time you pray, if your prayer is sincere, there will be a new feeling and new meaning in it, which will give you fresh courage, and you will understand that prayer is an education."

I can find no more apt description of the role of prayer for Sacred Heart University. Simply put, we pray because we are a learning community and prayer is a vital part of our education as Spirit-filled human beings. An institution of Catholic higher education, Sacred Heart University seeks to nourish not only the mind, but also the heart and the soul of each of its members. The practice of prayer, both silent and personal, shared and public, is central to this process. The prayers we say and the prayers we share shape us not only as individuals, but also as a community. This is especially true of the prayers collected in this volume. Old and new, traditional and innovative, they provide a glimpse of how the members of this Catholic university community have challenged and continue to challenge each other to live as disciples of Jesus.

As with any Christian community, there have been times when our actions have fallen short of our ideals, and at these times we have prayed for forgiveness. There have been moments in our history when the complexity of the world has overwhelmed us, and we have asked for guidance. Whatever the situation or the occasion, it has been our prayer that has sustained us.

To read these prayers is to discover something about the heart of this community. If you meet persons who have ever-been associated with Sacred Heart University, even for a brief period of time, they will tell you that there is something special about this place. They will speak of a spirit, an intangible quality that, although hard to describe, made them feel immediately at home as soon when they arrived on campus. This spirit is rooted in our faith, and the prayers collected in this volume have grown out of that faith. These prayers are our stories: stories of challenge and struggle as we contemplate what it means to be a Catholic university in the 21st century, stories of gratitude as we recount the many blessings we receive, and stories of hope as we continue to discover the unique plan God has for each one of us.

I invite you to join our Sacred Heart University community in its prayer—and to come to know its spirit as I have been privileged to know it.

Anthony J. Cernera, Ph.D.
President

Table of Contents

Nothing is more practical than finding God,
that is, than falling in love in a quite absolute, final way.
What you are in love with,
what seizes your imagination,
will affect everything.
It will decide what will get you out of bed in the morning,
what you will do with your evenings,
how you will spend your weekends,
what you read, what you know that breaks your heart,
and what amazes you with joy and gratitude.
Fall in love, stay in love, and it will decide everything.

— *Pedro Arrupe, SJ (1907-1991)*

"Go confidently in the direction of your dreams."
— Henry David Thoreau

This book began as a dream. It was the dream of Sacred Heart University's president Anthony J. Cernera to one day welcome each new student with a book of prayers. It would not be a traditional prayerbook, although it would draw heavily from the rich heritage of the Catholic prayer tradition. Nor would it be an ornamental book, something to adorn a shelf or put on a table only when one's parents were in town. This book, comprised mainly of original prayers by members of our community, would be a true companion for the journey of college life. A friend, with many pages that one could turn to over and over again in times of difficulty or when inspiration was needed, this book would be food for the soul.

It was a bold dream, and those of us who were first approached to work on the project were both intrigued and intimidated by the prospect of putting together such a collection. Would our students and staff be willing to share their personal prayers in a book such as this? Would these prayers speak to the heart of the University experience? Would they speak to our students' hearts? These were the questions that initially concerned us, but as we prayed and invited others to pray with us, our fears were quickly allayed. To our delight we discovered that many members of our community were glad to take part in a project such as this, and over the course of a year the dream became a reality.

When I first read the prayers collected in this volume, I expected them to touch my heart. I expected to be moved. I did not expect to be changed, and yet, changed is exactly what I have become. For contained in these humble pages are dozens of intimate conversations with God, simple prayers written by ordinary men and women in love with God, seeking answers to some of life's most perplexing questions. To *read* these prayers is to discover something very special about the heart of this community. As I myself have discovered, to *pray* these prayers is to open oneself up to the possibility of being changed by them, by the people who wrote them, and the love that inspired them.

As the manuscript evolved, our hearts became light, for we heard God's voice anew in the words of our colleagues, friends and students. The voice beckoned us toward a new reality and challenged us to break through artificial barriers that sometimes separate us—student/teacher, employee/employer, faculty/staff—and to see ourselves as God sees us, as sisters and brothers. It was as if the pages themselves began to say: "Welcome, Reader. You are not the first to walk this way. Many have come before you and many pray with you now. Join your song with ours and give glory to God."

The process of assembling the book was also a graced experience filled with surprises. First, we collected the prayers we use to mark special occasions in the University's life, those public moments such as "moving-in" day, Founder's Day, and graduation. Public prayers such as these say something about who we are as a community. They tell our story, renew our spirit, and challenge us to live as God's people.

Next, we invited members of the University community to share their private moments of prayer. These prayers are more personal and reflect the individual's relationship with God. They include a professor's prayer before teaching and a young man's prayer before a date. The intimacy of these selections helps us to remember that prayers are more than just texts: they are living encounters between the ones who pray and the God to whom they pray.

Finally, we included some traditional prayers from our rich Catholic heritage along with bits of wisdom from some of our favorite saints and mystics. These selections remind us that, as disciples of Jesus, our community extends beyond the University to include all those who have gone before us.

When the time came to name this collection, we asked ourselves, "Where does prayer come from? The soul? The spirit?" Sacred Scripture speaks most often of the *heart*; in fact the Bible mentions the "heart" more than one thousand times. It is the heart that prays, and it is the heart that is God's chosen dwelling place. The prayers you will find in this volume come from *our* hearts. We hope they will be prayers that you can use and prayers that you can live. Let them fill your soul as they have filled ours. They are our gift to you. May your prayer be your gift to us.

Patricia Leonard Pasley
Editor

Feast of the Transfiguration
August 6, 2002

How to Use This Book

This book is designed to be picked up and put down often,
leaving time and space for silent reflection.

Pause often, return often,
and allow God to enter into your praying
as well as into your quiet time,
filling them both with grace.

Come to this book expectantly.
Come to have truths revealed.
Come unhurried.
Come with an open heart.
Come, even if nothing seems to
come from your coming,
and receive the gift of prayer.

A Reader's Blessing

Bless you, Reader.
In these pages may you discover
a wisdom you can use
and a song your soul can sing.
May this book become for you
a companion on your journey
and a lamp to light your way.
With every prayer you read
and every prayer you live,
may your path become clearer,
your joy more complete,
and God's plan for you unfold
exactly as it should.
Amen.

Good and gracious God,
from the beginning of time
you have called each and every one of us
to fullness of life with you
and with one another.
You have shown us the path of life
and invite us each day
to learn the truth that your word is for us.
Bless this University community
named in honor of your Jesus's sacred heart.
Help us to realize that
we are made in your image and likeness
and that each of us is your beloved daughter or son.
Give us the grace to know what it is
that we are called to do with our lives,
and grant us the humility
to keep our hearts and minds open
to the voice of your Holy Spirit.
Amen.

– Anthony J. Cernera, Ph.D.
President, Sacred Heart University

1. Prayers rising from University life

These original prayers were written

to mark special times and situations in the University's life.

There are prayers for public moments like graduation,

Founder's Day or a musical performance.

There are also prayers rising from

more personal experiences like

becoming a senior, going on a date

or taking a test.

Whether public or private,

shared or solitary,

prayer is an important part of the

Sacred Heart University way of life.

To the Sacred Heart of Jesus

Devotion to the physical heart of Jesus is a practice that can be traced back to the Middle Ages. Today the symbol of the Sacred Heart and the love that it inspires continue to guide our University community. Here we offer some traditional prayers to the Sacred Heart of Jesus and one of our own.

O Heart of Love, I put all my trust in you.
For I fear all things from my own weakness,
but I hope for all things from your goodness.
Amen.

— Saint Margdret Mary Alacoque (1647-1690)

How good and pleasant it is
to dwell in the Heart of Jesus!
Who is there who does not love
a heart so wounded?
Who can refuse a return of love
to a heart so loving?

— Saint Bernard of Clairvaux (1090-1153)

9

O make my heart beat with your heart!
— *John Henry Cardinal Newman (1801-1890)*

O Sacred Heart of Jesus,
you have called me
to this place that bears your name,
and yet I am afraid.
When I do not know what to do
or where to turn,
let me turn to you, Lord.
Be my chapel here.
Direct my feet:
your path is my joy.
Enlighten my mind:
your teaching is my delight,
Open my ears:
your voice will comfort me.
Guide me
so that my every action
will help to realize your kingdom
and reflect a soul in love with God.
Amen.

— *Campus Ministry*

For Those Who Love Wisdom

Asking for God's guidance and wisdom before beginning the day's work or the day's study is a common theme in the prayers of our professors and students. Here are some of our favorites.

Dear Lord,
give me the strength to endure the challenges that lie ahead,
for it is only you who know what my future is.
Provide me with the wisdom I need
to make the right decisions for my life,
for it is only you who know why I am here.
Lead me to the right path,
the path illumined by your light.
Whether I falter or succeed,
give me the will to continue on my journey
Amen.

— Keith Smolinski, '02

"Prayer is the contemplation of the facts of life from the highest point of view."
— Ralph Waldo Emerson (1803-1882)

For Those Who Teach

Creator,
you are the source of all Life,
all Truth,
and all Beauty.

Bless me with
FAITH,
for wisdom of self is rooted in faith
and educated in mind.

Bless me with
LOVE,
a calling to be compassionate in heart
to all those I encounter along the path.

Bless me with
TRUTH,
the commitment to a justice grown from truth
and the courage to respond
to an ever-changing world

Bless me with
PEACE
To witness the unfolding souls of my students
as I accompany them along their way.

— Dr. Jeanne S. Marcato
Assistant Professor of Education

Before Exams

O God,
Source of all wisdom,
help me to use my time and my intelligence wisely
as I prepare for my exams.

Give me insight and understanding, a full grasp of the subject matter,
a good memory, and an ability to explain clearly what I have understood.

Help me to keep things in balance and not to become too anxious,
so that my work may truly reflect all that I have learned.

Bless my efforts with success,
and show me ways to use the knowledge I've gained
so that I may help in transforming our world for your greater glory.

Amen.

— Campus Ministry

"My child, keep sound wisdom and prudence; and they will be life for your soul."
— Proverbs 3:21-22

I Look Upon the Face of God

Lord, I look for you each day.
I pray my special thoughts and needs to you.
I have confidence that you hear,
even if, in your great wisdom,
you sometimes do not act.

I hope to know you better,
to hear your words,
to live my life in ways
that make you smile.
I long to see your face.

Help me to remember that, each day,
I see you in the classroom,
in the residence hall,
in the cafeteria,
and on the playing fields.

Remind me that you are here,
in the students and faculty,
the staff and visitors to our University.

Help me to see you each day in those I meet,
in those with whom I speak,
in those to whom I listen.
Remind me that your greatness, in some small part,
is in each and every one of these others.

Help me to see that glimpse of greatness,
and love them the way that I love you.
Remind me that I look upon the face of God
each and every day.
Amen.

— Dr. Michael J. Emery,
Associate Professor of Physical Therapy

"Your face, Lord, do I seek. Do not hide your face from me."
— Psalm 27:8-9

Grant Us Wisdom

Dear Lord,
in humility, we ask that you grant us
the wisdom to guide our students
to become people of conscience,
integrity and good will.

Help us, Lord, to be examples of professionalism.
Grant us patience to understand our students.
Help us to remember
how difficult the experience of college life can be.
Help us to encourage the love of learning.
Remind us daily, Lord, that our students deserve
our attention and our respect.
Forgive us when we fall short of our duty to them.

Please, Lord,
protect us from our own arrogance.
Help us to remember
that we, too, are students,
still learning our craft,
still making mistakes along the way,
and that our students can often be our teachers.

We ask this in the name of Jesus, our Savior.
Amen.

— Dr. Shirley A. Pavone
Assistant Professor of Psychology

"I pray because God is God."
— Dr. Margaret A. Palliser, OP
Assistant Vice President for Mission

Today I Teach

Dear Lord,

Today I teach.

Thank you for this opportunity to form and inform the minds of my students, for the chance to foster new thinkers able to shape a better world. Help me, Lord, to be conscious of the great power I possess. Lead me to use that power in the pursuit of truth with my students and for their best interest. In pursuing truth, we pursue you. As we seek you in truth, help us become a community of learners reflecting the highest human ideals.

Among the mundane activities, the inactive learners, the uncorrected papers, the long office hours, and the challenging relationships, help me to remember the gift of the vocation to teach. I am privileged to awaken intellects, to lead in questioning, to rejoice in insights.

Each day help me to strive for excellence so that I will be a worthy model for my students and a contributing colleague for my peers. Give me a joyful heart enriched by an awareness of your bountiful blessings and guided by the Spirit of truth. Amen.

— Dr. Thomas V. Forget
Vice President for Academic Affairs

For Special Intentions

Classes, departments, programs, teams and other groups will often write and use prayers that address their special hopes and concerns. Here are some that speak to us.

A New Student's Prayer

Dear Lord,
when I feel unknown and small remind me to stop . . .
and remember that you are here in this new place
and that your hand is gently guiding me
through this new time in my life.
Remind me that your love has brought me this far
and your love will carry me the rest of the way.
Let me be brave enough to be my true self,
strong enough to let others see my fear,
and smart enough to admit that I don't have all the answers.
Give me the wisdom that comes from uncertainty
and the holiness that comes from admitting my sins.
My feet are firmly planted on this path;
let it be the one you want me to follow.

— Patricia Leonard Pasley
Campus Minister

A goal of the Residential Life program is to help each student who lives on campus to feel at home. Vital to the success of this program is the hard work and dedication of more than sixty resident assistants. R.A.'s, as they are known, serve the needs of nearly 2,000 students a year at Sacred Heart University. Here is their prayer.

A Resident Assistant's Prayer

Holy and loving God,
we praise you for the life that you have given us.
We thank you for the gift of service that you have modeled for us,
and we ask you for the strength to become servants
to all those whom you place before us.

May we always remember that our first vocation is that of a student.
So help us, Lord, to become
     scholars of your wisdom and truth,
     studiers of your word,
     stewards of your creation,
     and promoters of your peace.

May the Holy Spirit show us what is the true nature of a servant leader
so that when we are in doubt, our hearts will be open to the knowledge that:

although we are not ordained ministers,
    we do minister to the needs of those in our halls;
although we are not licensed counselors,
    we do counsel those who are looking for someone who will listen;
although we are not doctors,
    we do help to heal the brokenness in the lives of those we meet;
although we are not lawyers,
    we do defend the rights of our students;
although we are not police officers,
    we do make the halls a safe place for all those who live there;
although we are not related family members,
    we do build a community to strengthen our relationships; and
although we are not saviors,
    we do, through our words and deeds, point the way to the Savior.

Holy and loving God,
we praise you for our keen and inquisitive minds.
We thank you for your grace that overlooks our mistakes,
and we ask you to help us to remember
that the harvest is plentiful but the workers are few.

We ask all these things through Christ, our everlasting Lord.
Amen.

— Allen J. Thomas Machielson
Assistant Director of Residential Life

A Student Leader's Prayer

Dear God,

Thank you for the opportunity to serve
as a leader of this community.
You are infinite in wisdom and in love.
I ask you to lead me.
May my service bring glory to you.

May I always put the needs of the community
before my own.
When there is a dispute, grant me wisdom
to establish justice.
When there is evil, grant me courage
to stand up for what is right.

With humility, Jesus washed the feet of his disciples.
With infinite trust and obedience to your word,
our Blessed Mother asked that your will be done.
With love and mercy, Mother Teresa opened her arms
to welcome the poor and destitute.
I ask for a small portion of these gifts
so that I may serve as you have commanded.

Amen.

— Thomas Pesce, '03
President of Student Government

"The Lord does not see as mortals see;
they look on the outward appearance,
but the Lord looks on the heart."
— 1 Samuel 16:7

A Sophomore's Prayer

(and for all those who find themselves feeling both wise and foolish from time to time)

Dear Lord,
we long to know your plan for us but fear the consequences
such a revelation may have for our everyday lives.
We want you to be close,
but only if we can choose the distance between us.
We are a paradox, Lord,
a mixture of wisdom and folly,
drawn to the cross but afraid of its price.
Still you find something to love about us.
We can be dull, yet we have moments of brilliance.
We are weak, yet we have demonstrated strength in times of adversity.
We are fragmented, leading lives that appear false (even to us),
yet we have the potential for wholeness and truth.

And through all of our contradictions,
you find something to love.
And your love
brightens what is dull,
strengthens what is weak,
enriches what is poor,
and makes whole what is broken.
May we always choose you,
God of paradoxes,
lover of unfinished projects,
lover of us
and all that we can be.
Amen.

— Patricia Leonard Pasley
Campus Minister

"Prayer is my way of communicating with God.
It uplifts my spirits in times of joy and sadness."
— Senior biology major

For a Student of the Health Sciences

Gracious God,
you who know me,
you who love me,
I ask for your guidance this day:

When I do not know if this is my calling,
I ask for discernment
that I may hear your voice
and carry out your will.

When I am overwhelmed
at the amount of information I must learn,
I ask for perseverance
and for trust
that what seems impossible alone
is possible with you.

When I am discouraged
and it seems that I will always be a student,
I ask for gratitude
for the opportunity that I have been given.
And I ask for courage to work
so that I can give back even more
than I have been given.

And when the sick and broken do come to me,
may I see only you.
Through my words, may you comfort them.
Through my hands, may you heal them.
And may I become invisible
so that they will know only you in their hour of need.

— Kevin R. Leonard Pasley, P.A.

A Couple's Prayer

Dear God,
throughout our lives we have turned to you
for comfort, strength, and hope.

We come before you not as individuals,
but as two people united because of your love.

We ask you to bless our relationship
as it continues to grow.
From boyfriend and girlfriend to an engaged couple,
we have chosen each other as life partners.

We acknowledge our separate prayerful ways,
but we desire to create a spiritual bond as a couple.
Grant us the ability to share our Christian lives
in union with you.
Help us to be open to this change.
Through our faith we ask this.
Amen.

– Darlene Harris, '00 and Michael Koosa, '00
(Wedding Date – July 19, 2003)

"It is also good to love: because love is difficult.

For one human being to love another human being:

that is perhaps the most difficult task that has been entrusted to us,

the ultimate task, the final test and proof,

the work for which all other work is merely preparation.

That is why young people,

who are beginners in everything,

are not yet capable of love:

it is something they must learn."

— Rainer Maria Rilke (1875-1926)

Athletics are an important part of Sacred Heart University life. Over sixty percent of our students are involved in some type of intercollegiate or intramural sports. Competitions, of all kinds, often begin with a prayer.

A Coach's Prayer

Lord, hold our student athletes in your loving hands.
Look after and protect them
in their competitions and travel.
Grant them the courage, honor, strength,
good sportsmanship, and skill needed
to successfully compete.
Inspire them in ways in which
they can make a difference
in our community and in our world.
Bless them and their parents
who share their sons and daughters with us
in a selfless commitment of service and time,
for they are the heart of this campus.
Lord, bless them and keep them from all harm
in their pursuit of excellence on our behalf.
Amen.

– C. Donald Cook
Director of Athletics

An Athlete's Prayer

Dear God,
Please give me your strength not to succumb to pain.
Allow me to continue to believe
that through your power I can do anything.
Please help me to focus my energy
into the wonderful gift you have given me.
Remind me that the physical pain will diminish
and the glory of overcoming it will remain forever.
Thank you for blessing me
with the love and support of my teammates.
With your grace, I give it my all.
Amen.

— *Lauren Honan, '03*

A Musician's Prayer

O Creator of all that is beautiful,
strengthen us with your love
and empower us with your grace
so that your life-giving word
may be proclaimed in our music and song.
Bless our instruments and voices
so that they may reflect your beauty
and give praise to you forever.
Amen.

— Keith Smolinski, '02

"The one who sings prays twice."
— Saint Augustine of Hippo (354-430)

An Intern's Prayer

(A prayer for those who are working as clinical interns, student teachers, or graduate assistants.)

Dear God,
I know what I want,
I know where I am going,
but I am not there yet.
This in-between phase, this limbo
of doing something but not exactly
my true destiny is so confusing.
I know being here is a learning experience,
but being here is not being there.
Will I ever really get there?
Please give me the strength to trust
this path I'm on and guide me
in conquering my fears and achieving my goals.
Amen.

— Angela Paulone, '01
Graduate Assistant, Campus Ministry

"Grant us grace, Almighty Father, so to pray as to deserve to be heard."
— Jane Austen (1775-1817)

A Senior's Prayer

Lord,
do not let me leave this place unchanged.
Give me new eyes to see
how interesting and beautiful
is the work of shaping
the course of my life.
Set my feet on a holy path.
Instill in me an imagination for the sacred,
an imagination that demands
that my dreams be fleshed out
in concrete actions
of justice and love.
Thank you for having been with me
during this time of preparation
for the work that lies ahead.
Now leave with me.
With you by my side, I am ready.
Fill me with your Spirit,
then set me free.
Amen.

— Campus Ministry

"We need to learn ways of praying which are compatible
with the maturing of our minds and our faith . . . .
No one should be content to remain at one level in the life of prayer,
nor should we abandon prayer even when . . . prayer seems impossible.
When we do not know how or what to pray, this too should be part of our prayer."

— Perry LeFevre

An Alumni Prayer

O God,
your infinite wisdom flows into my heart,
and my soul is constantly nourished by it.

> I always thought my path was clear, straight . . .
> then I graduated. Oh, my, how the path turns.

I do the work I am called to do,
It's challenging, rewarding, fun.
(I even pay the bills.)

> Then I begin to feel lost.
> Work is not rewarding.
> Have you left me?
> Where is my path?
> Where is my guide?

I step back, focus, and realize
that your love never faltered –
it was just that my road needed to turn.

With your love and my faith
my journey continues, changes,
and leads me to grow.
Stay close.
Amen.

– Cara Broussard, '98

"Certain thoughts are prayers. There are moments when,
whatever be the attitude of the body, the soul is on its knees."
– Victor Hugo (1802-1885)

Many groups on campus—departments, athletic teams, clubs, organizations, sororities and fraternities — like to begin their gatherings with prayer.

"Where Two or Three Are Gathered"

God of unconditional love and unlimited promise,
Thank you for the incredible abundance of gifts you have given to us in each other—
     amazing gifts to be used in the service of others.
Give us the courage, honesty, and humility we need to be an even more effective team.
Help us to remember why we are here—
          to be reflections of your love for each other
          and for all of the members of our University community,
          signs of hope and healing, events of compassion and mercy.

We pray for the members of our community who are in special need at this time,
          those whom we know well and those whose needs are hidden from us,
          those whose pain we have seen but have not acknowledged,
          and especially those whose pain we cannot know, those who remain mysteries to us:
                    All who are discouraged.
                    All who feel unappreciated or unrespected.
                    All who are afraid.
                    All whom we find difficult.
                    All whom we ourselves have frustrated or hurt.

We ask your forgiveness and each other's forgiveness,
      You know the reasons and need for this request even better than we do.
      Help us to find the words and the ways to be forgiveness and hope for each other,
      to let go of any misunderstandings or failures in kindness that we have experienced.

You have given us the commandment to love one another.
Help us to do that,
      to love one another—
      not in the abstract,
      but in the concrete and complex reality of each day—
      because without love, we are but clanging cymbals.
We know this, but we really need to remind ourselves.
      Thank you for this opportunity to be re-mindful
            —mindful of you once again!

Amen.

– Dr. Margaret A. Palliser, OP
Assistant Vice President for Mission

An Administrator's Prayer
"When I Have Too Much To Do"

When I have too much to do,

help me to turn to you, my God.

Give me insight into what is important at this moment—

grant me courage to face challenges . . .

compassion as I listen to others . . .

perseverance to tackle difficult tasks . . .

peace in all things.

Above all, help me, my God, to remember that it is your work

that I am about—not mine.

Amen.

— Dr. Donna Dodge, SC
Vice President for Mission and Planning

"Those who pray as well as work at the tasks they have to do, and combine their prayer with suitable activity, will be praying always. That is the only way in which it is possible never to stop praying."

— Origen (185-254)

Co-Workers' Prayer

You have placed us on the same path of life,
strangers walking side by side in this blessed space and time;
sharing our daily bread and tasks, we dare to trust and respect each other
and grow in love and friendship.

You inspire us with your wisdom and light our way,
companions on the journey, a family of faith;
on the road, we support and encourage one another to learn and grow,
and we embrace each other's sorrows and joys.

Thank you, Lord, for bringing us together in community;
guide our hearts and minds as we work together to achieve our goals.
Teach us to celebrate your presence in each person
so that we might be signs of your peace.

— *Carol-Anne Dabek*
Office Manager, Campus Ministry

A Supervisor's Prayer

O God,
it's another day,
filled with its unique challenges
and opportunities to serve.

Thank you for everything just the way it is,
fertile ground for your miracles of grace.

As I try to lead,
help me to be a servant—
respectful and mindful
of my colleagues' gifts and needs,
strengths and weaknesses,
hopes and dreams,
worries and fears.

Help me to be objective and fair,
honest and straightforward,
collegial and inclusive,
supportive and encouraging.
Help me to listen attentively
and to respond with respect.

Give me the right words,
good timing, patience,
and a sense of humor
as I go about the business
of getting business done.

If I do a really good job today,
no one will notice me.
Help me to remember that!
And help me not merely to allow others to shine,
but to find ways to celebrate their successes.

May I embrace today's tasks
with confidence, optimism, and enthusiasm.
And when I feel discouraged,
remind me that you are with me.

Amen.

— Dr. Margaret A. Palliser, OP
Assistant Vice President for Mission

The good leader is the one whom the people revere.
The great leader is the one about whom the people say, "We did it ourselves."
— Lao Tzu (6th Century B.C.)

for Special Days and Special Occasions

Marking special moments in University life is often done with prayer.

As We Begin a New Semester (Teachers)

Dear Lord,
as we begin this new semester,
grant us peace, tolerance and grace.
Teach us, Father, to respect all pathways that lead to you.
Help us to be your instruments as we guide our students.
Our prayer is that they become wise, loving, professional people
with an appreciation of family, community, self and, most of all, faith.
Watch over us, dear Lord, as we begin this journey.
Amen.

– Dr. Shirley A. Pavone
Assistant Professor of Psychology

As We Begin a New Semester (Students)

Dear Lord,
as we begin this new semester,
grant us peace, tolerance and grace.
Teach us, Father, to respect all pathways that lead to you.
Help us to be your instruments as we learn and grow.
Our prayer is that we become wise, loving and professional people
with an appreciation of family, community, self and, most of all, faith.
Watch over us, dear Lord, as we begin this journey.
Amen.

— *Dr. Shirley A. Pavone*
Assistant Professor of Psychology

Moving-In Day

O God, what was I thinking?
Last week I couldn't wait,
and now—maybe it's not for me.
    Saying "good-bye" to my family,
    my friends . . . .
    I can't believe that my whole life
    fits into a few boxes.
        God, please don't leave me.
        You are my comfort,
        my foundation.
            With you, I think I am ready,
            ready to grow,
            ready to learn,
            almost ready to find out who I am.
                Help me to be steady on my path
                Help me to stay in your light.

                        – *Cara Broussard, '98*

"Prayer begins where human capacity ends."
    – Norman Vincent Peale (1898-1993)

Sacred Heart University was founded in 1963 by The Most Reverend Walter W. Curtis, Second Bishop of Bridgeport. Each year the University gathers to commemorate this important moment in its history with a celebratory luncheon. The celebration, of course, begins with prayer.

Founder's Day Prayer

Good and gracious God, we thank you for the many gifts you have given us:
the energy and enthusiasm that first created and now sustains
this community of learning and faith;
the perseverance and the courage that help us to reflect
and to change along the way;
the vision and the commitment to embrace our mission of service
to our students and to the community;
the willingness to discuss and collaborate,
and sometimes to disagree and compromise,
as we face the challenges of our future.
May your Spirit continue to move among us,
to inspire our work and teaching,
to inform our decisions,
and to lead us to answer your call
as your witnesses and disciples in this world.
Amen.

— *Dr. Michelle Lusardi*
Associate Professor of Physical Therapy

47

Before a Performance

In prayer, as in many long-term relationships, the participants develop shorthand for communication. E.g., conversation with my wife on a typical Monday evening: *"Did you remember?" "Yes." "Well, did you?" "Not yet." "Then when?" "OK, now."* (All this to get the garbage cans to the top of the driveway.)

My immediate preparation for a performance, a class, an important meeting, a test, etc., involves a variety of physical and emotional work, and always includes prayer. However, the shorthand has become very much like, *"Well, God, here we are again — You know the routine — Thanks."*

Dear Lord,
I am here by your grace.
My talents grow from what you have given me.
Thank you for those gifts.
I have worked hard to prepare for this moment.
Thank you for the energy and time to do that.
You will help me through any challenge.
Thank you for your loving support.
I surrender to your care.
Thank you.
I'll do my best.

There is, of course, the epilogue. Every performance has an end at which point one can know either success or failure. Each can be marked by prayer.

This result celebrates your glory.
Thank you for making me your tool.

Help me to learn and grow from this.
Thank you for this opportunity.

– *Dr. Edward W. Malin*
Associate Professor of Psychology

Before a Competition

O Lord,
On this day of friendly competition,
I ask you to bless us.
Make us strong competitors,
models of sportsmanship,
and ambassadors of good will.
As we embark on future endeavors,
I ask you to remind us of the joy
we have experienced in the win
and the wisdom we have gained
in the disappointment of a loss.
In all that we may achieve
on the field, in the ring, or on the courts,
guide us to become better human beings
and faithful Christians.
Amen.

– Brian Reardon
Head Wrestling Coach

Before a Date

Tonight, Lord, I ask you for your guidance and assistance on my date.

Tonight, Lord, I ask you to place your loving hand upon my shoulder and aid my courting.
Tonight, Lord, I ask you to instill in me dignity and respect.
Tonight, Lord, I ask you to instill in me confidence and poise.
Tonight, Lord, I ask you to instill in me wit and humor.
Tonight, Lord, I ask you to settle the tightness in my stomach and the nerves in my voice.
Tonight, Lord, I ask you to grant me the wisdom that only you have.
Tonight, Lord, please help my words be heard and understood as I wish them to be.
Tonight, Lord, please help my date to enjoy my company as much as I enjoy hers.

Tonight, Lord, I ask you for many things,
     and I ask you because you're the only one who can grant them to me.
Thank you, Lord, for hearing my prayer.
Thank you, Lord, for all that you have done for me.
Thank you, Lord, for all that you have been through with me.

Amen.

— Michael DiPietro, '02

"Prayer is emoting, singing, thinking, hoping, grieving, feeling, celebrating, and all-consuming."
— Donna Wilkins
Academic Associate to the Vice President for Academic Affairs

As a community within a larger community, we are grateful when a neighbor shares a prayer with us. This one comes from a local brewer who prays for our students who are learning to navigate in a new world of freedoms and choices when it comes to the use of alcohol.

Before I Celebrate

Dear Lord,
tonight I will be celebrating with my friends,
and I will be asked if I want a drink.
It is you who have given me the gift of free will,
and so it is you that I ask to guide my actions tonight.
If it is companionship or self-confidence I seek from the bottle,
help me to find these things in you.
If calmness or courage is what I'm looking for from a glass (or two),
give me the strength to find these things within myself.
And if I choose to have a drink tonight,
let me truly appreciate this gift in the way your Son did.
Let me honor my body and my mind
with choices that respect my health and spirit.
Keep me ever mindful of the power of alcohol,
and help those who have fallen under its spell
to find in you a greater power.
Amen.

— *Robert W. Leonard*

Friday Night Prayer

Dear Lord,
thank you for my wonderful friends and family.
As I prepare to go out tonight, I feel stronger knowing
that you have given me the values that I need to make healthy, moral decisions.
O Lord, tonight and always, guide me to make responsible choices.
Help me to remain strong in saying "no" to the negative influences I may encounter.
Help me to refrain from substances that will harm or impair my judgment.
Protect those whom I will socialize with, and give them clear judgment.
Remind me that my safety and the safety of those around me
should come before any other decision that I make.
As I go out tonight, I will remember the valuable lessons you have taught me.
With your assistance, I will make the best decisions I can,
not only for myself, but for all those whom I love as well.
Amen.

— Meredith LaParle, '02
Senior Resident Assistant

Blessings are prayers that ask for God's gifts for various individuals or groups. Every baptized person is called to be a "blessing" and also to bless.

When We Gather to Share a Meal

God of creation, God of love,
we ask your blessing on this meal.
As we gather to celebrate,
may this meal nourish us
not only in body,
but in mind and spirit,
so that we may become nourishment
for one another.
Amen.

— *Noëlle D'Agostino*
Campus Minister

Pray for peace, and grace, and spiritual food,
For wisdom and guidance—for all these. are good,
But don't forget the potatoes.
— Rev. John Tyler Pettee (1822-1907)

Lord, we invite you to this table;
join the circle we have made.
Be the food that makes us strong;
be the path our feet are on.
Be compassion in every dealing
with a sister or a brother.
Be the love that now enfolds us,
binding us to one another.
Be strength to face our problems,
whatever they may be.
Be our blessing, Lord and Father—
in your grace we are set free.

— Campus Ministry

Graduation Blessings

God of wisdom, bless these graduates
whose hearts you have fashioned
for beauty and grace.
Bless those who love them
and those who have guided them
to this holy time and place.
Call them to discovery,
to seek their truest self,
to fall in love with wisdom
and claim her as their wealth.
Send them forth in knowledge,
your teachings to be their guide.
Watch over them,
protect them,
walk softly by their side.
Amen.

— Campus Ministry

"Prayer is the highest achievement of which the human person is capable."
— Saint Edith Stein (1891-1942)

May God give you strength
and a virtuous heart,
so that in time of trial
you will find yourself armed with treasures you can use.
> May God give you faith,
> so that in leaving this place,
> you know firmly and with conviction
> who made you, and why,
> and for what purpose.
>> May God give you peace, a lasting peace
>> that dwells in your heart
>> and enables you to comprehend
>> the breadth and length,
>> the height and depth of Christ's love for you.
>>> And one day soon, may God return you to us
>>> so that we may again rejoice in your goodness
>>> and give thanks for our time together.
>>> Amen.

— Campus Ministry

57

For and by Parents

For My Parents As I Begin College

Loving God,

I thank you for my mother,
in whom I lived,
and moved,
and had my being.

I thank you for my father,
who loves me enough to let me go,
but never to leave me.

From their love, my life began;
with their support,
this new adventure of college begins.
Watch over them, God,
in this time of change.

Help me to respect my Mom's and Dad's concerns
and to be open to their counsel.
Remind me that ours is a partnership
based on love and support.

Thank you for all of the blessings
you have bestowed upon me,
especially my mother and father,
in whose love I have abundant gifts
and everything I need to succeed
in this new time in my life.
Amen.

— Regina Dempsey, '04

"We pray as we live, because we live as we pray."
— Catechism of the Catholic Church, No. 2725

Watch Over Our Child

Heavenly Father, watch over and protect our child as she leaves our home to embark on a new path of learning and independence. Be her strength when decisions face her. Let her faith and her family's love provide an anchor for her. Help her to enjoy her new freedoms, to keep safe, and to make good choices.

Give us the wisdom to be silent when it is best and to speak when it is necessary. Let us be good listeners and have incredible understanding. Most of all, no matter what the situation, let us continue to provide unquestioning love.

Jesus, always be the Brother and Friend that our child will need. When friends disappoint her, when responsibilities overwhelm her, be there for her. Remind her of your life and the trials you endured. May your life and the loving relationships you enjoyed provide an inspiration for her.

As our child enters adulthood, help us to be friend as well as parent. Help us to celebrate with her the growth to womanhood and professionalism. Help us to be there whenever she calls.

Holy Spirit, enlighten our child that she may be academically successful. Fill her with your Divine Love so she may love herself and love all those she comes in contact with. Help her to become the best that she may be and share her gifts and talents with all.

Guide us as parents during rewarding and difficult times. Enlighten us with your wisdom. Help us to continue to enjoy our family. Let us have fun together and always support each other. Help each of us to continue to grow in love and grace. Amen.

— Kathy and Jack Dempsey
Parents of Regina Dempsey, '04

"Prayer is nothing but love."
— Saint Augustine of Hippo (354-430)

As Our Child's Journey Begins

Dear Lord,
we ask your blessing on our daughter as she
begins a new journey without our presence, but with yours.
We ask that you take her heart and mind and expand and explore
them to the depths with knowledge, values,
and life experiences that will enrich her mind and spirit.
Watch over her closely,
especially in the early months of this first year,
for the decisions will be challenging
and the support may be uncertain or unknown.
Let your strength and guidance join ours
to remind her that she will not always be the newest and the youngest,
and that this is the beginning of a new life,
new friends, and a new self.
Be with her, bless her as we do, and help her to remember
she remains always special in your heart and ours.
Amen.

— Sharon and Bob Broussard
Parents of Cara Broussard, '98

"A child who loves wisdom makes a parent glad."
— Proverbs 29:3

There are as many ways to pray
as there are moments in life.
Sometimes we seek out a quiet spot to be alone.
Sometimes we look for a friend
and want to be together.
Sometimes we like a book,
sometimes we prefer music.
Sometimes we want to sing out with hundreds,
sometimes only whisper with a few.
Sometimes we want to say it with a deep silence.
In all these moments,
we gradually make our lives more a prayer,
and we open our hands
to be led by God even to places
we would rather not go.

— *Henri Nouwen (1932-1996)*

To Begin and End the Day

When we first began this project we asked members of the University
community to share with us their favorite prayers. Time and time again,
the response we heard was, "Here is a prayer I use to start my day"
or, "Here is a prayer I say before I go to bed."
The many contributions of original and traditional prayers
reaffirmed for us the importance of the ancient tradition
of beginning and ending each day by praising God.
Here are some of our favorite morning and evening prayers.

Morning Offering

Dear Lord,
it's the start of a new day.
Be with me through the day.
Let my thoughts be pure,
my judgments be sincere,
and my words be kind.
May I treat others the
way I want to be treated.
Give me the strength to
make it through another day.
Amen.

– Michael E. Tompkins
Cleaning Supervisor, Buildings and Grounds

"The Lord used to speak to Moses face to face, as one speaks to a friend."
– Exodus 33:11

"In the morning, O Lord, you hear my voice:
in the morning I lay my requests before you and wait in expectation."
– Psalm 5:3 (from The New International Version)

In this holy moment
before the day begins,
I turn to you, O Lord, and ask:
shape the words in my mouth,
the actions of my body,
the thoughts of my mind.
Let everything
that comes from me
reflect the light
that comes from you.
Amen.

– Campus Ministry

May you be the God I serve today.
Let me follow no tempting other.
May I see your face revealed
in each sister and each brother.
Fill my words with wisdom.
Let my mouth sing out your praise.
Let my heart compose this love song;
Lord, be with me all my days.
Surround me with your blessing
as I begin this day's new tasks.
Touch me with your fire.
Love me. ~ Know me. ~ Move me.
This, O Lord, is all I ask.
Amen.

– Campus Ministry

"Rising in the morning I noticed that God laid the world at my feet."
— Corrine De Winter

Dear Lord,
as I begin this day,
guide me to make
the right decisions.
Help me to overcome
my everyday, fears and
grow in knowledge
and wisdom.
Amen.

— Christine Thorne, '02

Father, as I awake this morning,
I think about the day ahead of me.
Help me to notice all the beauty you have made.
Help me to see you in those around me
and to treat them the way I want to be treated,
because sometimes it is hard to do, Lord.
Help me to pay attention in my classes and do well on my tests.
Finally, and most important, help me to trust in you
and not spend my time worrying about things
because you will take care of everything.

— Amanda Astrella, '00

As The Day Ends

Father, bless us as we go our way
to follow different paths in different ways.

Charge us to put our love in action
and give us faith in abundant ration.

Help us to see you in each new face.
Let hatred and prejudice your love erase.

Bless us richly as we depart,
then guide us back to your Sacred Heart.

— Keysha Whitaker, '02

"I pray because it is a wonderful way for me to take a look at myself through God's
eyes. In this way I can see that I am a servant of God, trying to do his will.
When I pray, I have confidence that God will answer my prayers."
— Seamus Bradley, '05

Evening Praise for the Light

O joyful light of the holy glory of the immortal Father,
heavenly, holy, blessed Jesus Christ!
Now that we have come to the sun's hour of rest,
the lights of evening 'round us shine.
We praise the Father, the Son and the Holy Spirit,
One God.

Worthy are you, O Lord,
at all times to be praised with undefiled tongue,
O Son of God, O giver of life!
Therefore you are glorified throughout the universe.

— Traditional

Now I lay me down to sleep,
I pray the Lord my soul to keep;
If I should die before I wake,
I pray the Lord my soul to take.

— *New England Primer*
(18th century, based on
a manuscript from 1160 AD)

"I pray because it is a comfort to me.
I pray that I may rise the next day.
I pray because I have lost so many;
it is a way for me to feel closer to them
and to God."

— *Caitlin Moreira, '05*

Night Prayer

Watch, dear Lord,
with those who wake, or watch, or weep tonight,
and give your angels charge over those who sleep.

O Lord Jesus Christ,

Tend your sick ones.
Rest your weary ones.
Bless your dying ones.
Soothe your suffering ones.
Pity your afflicted ones.
Shield your joyous ones.
And all for your love's sake.

Amen.

– *Saint Augustine of Hippo (354-430)*

Sacred Time

One of the rich treasures of our Catholic tradition is the celebration of the liturgical year. Every year the Church puts before us the great mysteries of our faith through the various liturgical feasts and seasons.

Advent

Come, Lord, and make your dwelling here
among your people who long to see your face.

Come! O vulnerable child;
let our community be like Bethlehem of old,
a place where angels sing your praises
and simple shepherds contemplate your face.

Come, teach us greatness through simplicity of life.
Help us to live in the presence of your love.
When imitating you, may we help the world to see
the compassion you bring within your infant Heart.

– Fr. Gustavo A. Falla,
Campus Minister

Come, Lord Jesus.
Come quickly.
You know that I need you.
You know that we need you.

Come, Lord Jesus.
I suspect that I really don't understand what I'm asking for,
but don't let that stop you from coming!
Just help me to recognize you and welcome you
whenever and however you come.
Amen.

— Dr. Margaret A. Palliser, OP
Assistant Vice President for Mission

"Prayer need not always be vocal. It can be a more complete awareness and appreciation for the beauty with which God has surrounded us. Prayer helps us to look inward, to examine our lives more clearly, and makes us more aware of the things that truly matter."

— Loretta Winter
Assistant to the Chairs of the Departments of History,
Political Science, Philosophy and Religious Studies

"Because of his boundless love,
Jesus became what we are
that he might make us what he is."
— Saint Irenaeus (130-200)

Christmas

How we have longed for this day to celebrate your presence,
your becoming one like us in all but sin,
your bringing life and love and peace
to a world that has known so much darkness and death.

Best of all, you have come not for a short visit!
You have pitched a tent within our hearts,
giving us hope for a new life,
the possibility for eternal glory.

— Fr. Gustavo A. Falla
Campus Minister

Lent

O God, for forty days and nights
We journey through the desert to you, our heart's desire.
Wandering and wondering, "Are we there yet?"
Not there, now here, patient in this place.
Be our

> Angel of Life
> Staff against the serpents
> Rod that draws water from rock
> Bread from heaven
> Cloud of knowing-comfort
> Guide of grace
> Lamb of sacrifice
> Promise of peace.

Lead us to the banks of blooming, where
Manna is living memory
Wine is danced song
Dawn destroys death and
Your Word lights our home.

— Dr. David L. Coppola
Director of Conferences and Publications
Center for Christian-Jewish Understanding

Easter

O God,
We saw the bread crumbs, emptied vessels, damp towels
Scattered over the shaking floor of our faith.
Justice was swept under the rug of violence
And redemption hung in the balance of a cross.
Just when all seemed lost and death began to dance
The long night came to an end.
Dying you destroyed our death.

At dawn, on the first day of the week
We pulled ourselves away from tear-stained pillows
And walked in tired mourning to the place
Where unguarded, the stone, was rolled away,
Revealing an empty tomb
Full of life and possibility!
The earth shook with the news, "He is not here!"
Rising, You restored our life!

Light shines and lilies bloom.
You are with us again in this upper room.
We sigh and laugh at stories of darkness past.
At your table we eat and sing
Alleluia! Alleluia! Bells of blessing ring!
We dare to touch each other's hands and side.
Peace is your gift, Love is our guide.
Lord Jesus, come in glory!

— Dr. David L. Coppola
Director of Conferences and Publications
Center for Christian-Jewish Understanding

Pentecost

Spirit of life and wisdom, come.
Spirit of love and understanding, come.
Spirit of knowledge and truth, come.

Come into our lives and fill with your power
the hearts and minds of those who need you.

Fill our classrooms with your presence,
and let your love be communicated through our deeds.
Be our advocate and friend on our path to Christ.

Amen.

— Fr. Gustavo A. Falla
Campus Minister

Any Time

For many members of the Sacred Heart University community
prayer is a way of life, a form of communication
that allows us to find peace and stillness
in the midst of a busy day.
These prayers have risen from our everyday experiences.
Their subject matter and styles are as diverse as the authors themselves.
These are prayers from the heart.
They remind us that prayer should not be confined to
Sunday morning, grace before meals, or times of trouble.
These prayers are for any time because praying is living.

I Will

I will live this day in faith
and be thankful for all that I have.

I will know, Lord, that you have given me
the strength I need to accomplish all
that I have to do today.

I will follow you with my words,
with my actions,
and with every choice I make.

I will ask for a blessing for my friends,
for my family,
and for my community.

I will be your servant, Lord.
Amen.

— *Karen Craver, '02*

*"I will bless the Lord at all times; his praise shall continually be in my mouth.
My soul makes its boast in the Lord; let the humble hear and be glad."*

— Psalm 34:1-2

Thank You For Everything I Have

Dear Lord,
thank you for everything that I have.
Everyday of my life is filled with amazing blessings.
Thank you for the things I do not have,
for in their absence you have shown me
what it is that I truly need.
Thank you for giving me strength and perseverance.
When I achieve my goals, may I make you proud.
Thank you for showing me my limits,
for even when I fail, with you I can always try again.
Thank you for the times when you have worked through me
and led me to share your love with others.
Thank you for always forgiving me,
even when I don't do what you have shown me is right.
Thank you for hope and love,
faith, comfort and forgiveness,
and all the gifts I have found in you.
Amen.

— Greer Phillips, '02

Hear Me, O Lord

Hear me, O Lord.

Grant me the strength to lead
and the courage to follow.

Give me your hand to hold
and your shoulder to cry on.

Be my friend, my brother,
and my companion.

Most of all, Lord, just be there for me.

— Ryan Carlson, '02

"I thank you, my God, for having in a thousand different ways
led my eyes to discover the immense simplicity of things."
— Pierre Teilhard de Chardin, SJ (1881-1955)

Day by Day

Thanks be to you,
Lord Jesus Christ,
for all the benefits
that you have won for us
for all the pains and insults
that you have borne for us.
O most merciful Redeemer,
Friend and Brother,
may we know you more clearly,
love you more dearly,
follow you more nearly,
day by day.

— Richard de Wych, Bishop of Chichester (1197-1253)

"Prayer is freedom and affirmation growing out of nothingness into love. Prayer is the flowering of our inmost freedom, in response to the Word of God. Prayer is not only dialogue with God: it is the communion of our freedom with his ultimate freedom, his infinite spirit."
— Thomas Merton (1910-1968)

83

The Lord is near. Do not worry about anything."
– Philippians 4:6

What Should I Do with My Life?

Hi, God. Here I am again.
I know you love me enough to listen to me,
so here's what I'm thinking about:
what the heck should I do with my life?
I've thought a lot about it—
get a good job that I would like doing, with a decent salary;
get married (sooner or later?) and be a good parent.
I know these are all good things
and that you'd love it, love me if I did them.
I need your help finding and choosing the right job,
the best spouse.

Then, there's that other possibility,
the one that I can't imagine saying "yes" to.
It's crazy to even say the words:
be a priest, religious brother, sister?
Could you even do that to me?
Want me in one of those vocations?
If you do, and if I opt for something else,
you'll still love me more than I can imagine!

Just for the fun of it, toss out your opinion,
give me a little clue.
I might buy into it, I might not—
either because I'm too scared
or because I just don't like the idea.
But it would be good to at least understand each other
and then go on being friends.

Amen.

— Fr. Robert Malone, CSC
Campus Minister

Help Me, Lord, to Be the Best Person I Can Be

Dear God,
      please help me to be the best person I can be.
Help me to understand my thoughts and feelings.
Help me to be a good friend.
Help me to understand my friends' thoughts and feelings.
Help me to not be angry with others or myself when I don't understand.
Help me to be unselfish and charitable.
Help me to recognize my role in all of the communities I am a part of
      and to serve you to the best of my ability.
Help me to fulfill my duties as a daughter, a friend,
      a student, a volunteer, and a Christian.
Help me to love and accept all the people around me.
Help me to love you above all things, to see you in everything I encounter,
      and to strive for my own deeper understanding of you.
Amen.

– Keri Nastri, '03

"I delight to do your will, O my God; your law is within my heart!"
      – Psalm 40:8

Make Us Attentive to Your Word

Heavenly Father,
make us attentive to your Word,
grateful for the gifts you have given us,
and sorry for the times we have taken
your generosity for granted.

Open our hearts
to receive your good news.
Let us hear your voice so that
your will becomes
increasingly clear to us
with the passing of each new day.

Charge us to see the good in all people;
hold us accountable when we don't.
Let justice be our goal
and your everlasting love
the only reward we seek.

Thank you for your blessings and
for filling our lives with good things,
the greatest of which is your presence
inside each one of us.
Amen.

— *Debra Ventunelli, '00*

A Prayer to the COOL GOD

All those other people think they know you.
They think incense, candles, pictures, statues.
They think churches, folded hands, stuffy indoors.

But I know who you are:
outdoors, action;
indoors, absolute quiet;
really big, everything;
really small, so I can embrace you, and you me.

You're my very best friend,
my impossible lover!

You're COOL.

— Fr. Robert Malone, C.S.C.
Campus Minister

Father, Help Us

Heavenly Father,
help us to clear our minds of all things not from you.
Let your Holy Spirit move within us.
Give us the right words to say
and a comforting touch.

Strengthen us so that we may carry our own burdens
and shine your rays of hope upon those in need.
Grant us the wisdom to know your will,
and show us how to share it.
May your love fill us all.
In Christ's name we pray.
Amen.

— Sean Hatch, '04

"To me, prayer is a one-on-one conversation with God. It allows for expression of
one's concerns, wishes, intentions, and thoughts with privacy and without judgment."
— Stefanie L. Basciano, '04

A Prayer for Any Day

Help me to live this day
quietly and easily;
to lean upon your great strength
trustfully and restfully;
to wait for the unfolding of your will
patiently and serenely;
to meet others
peacefully and joyously;
and to face tomorrow
confidently and courageously.

– Author unknown

*"Because I am a woman involved in practical cares, I cannot give the first-half of
the day to these things but must meditate when I can, early in the morning and
on the fly during the day. Not in the privacy of a study—but here, there and
everywhere—at the kitchen table, on the train, on the ferry, on my way to and
from appointments and even while making supper or putting Teresa to bed."*
– Dorothy Day (1897-1980)

All shall be well
and all shall be well,
and all manner of thing
shall be well.

– Julian of Norwich (1342-c.1416)

A university, like any community,

is not immune to sorrow or suffering.

It is perhaps in times of difficulty and struggle

that our thoughts turn most easily to prayer.

"Lord, help me"

is perhaps the only prayer

we need during these times,

but here in the following pages

we offer you a few more.

When I Cannot Pray

When I cannot pray,
let me be silent.
If I cannot be silent,
let me ask "Lord, where are you when I need you?"
When no answer comes to satisfy my weary heart,
let me have the courage to be like Job,
to raise my hands towards the heavens
and scream, "What gives?"
If still I do not hear your voice,
let me hope.
If hope is more than I can manage,
then let me be silent.
When I can no longer be silent,
Lord, help me to pray.
Amen.

– *Patricia Leonard Pasley*
Campus Minister

"How is it that,
when there is so little time
to enjoy your presence,
you hide from me?"
– *Saint Teresa of Avila (1515-1582)*

Lord, What Do I Do?

Lord,
What do I do?
Where do I go?
What have I done?
How do I start again?
My love for you is great, but my actions do not show it;
my human, flawed side bullies me, and I let it win.
Not that I want it to take over,
but I feel no inner peace to carry me through.
I'm not a quitter, but I'm giving up.
I'm not a bad person, but I'm doing no good.
I know you're out there calling me and knocking on my door,
but I'm not answering.
I'm in a position to do your work,
but how can I guide when I am lost?
Not lost on my path, just lost in my heart.

My Lord, forever patient with these silly struggles,
What do I do?
Where do I go?
What have I done?
How do I start again?
I know I know the answers, but I just need to hear them.
Actually, you probably have shown me,
    but I wasn't watching or listening.
My eyes want to be open.
My ears want to hear.
My heart wants to spark and rekindle that flame.
I'm opening the door to let you in—
Welcome. I'm sorry it took so long to answer.

— Angela Paulone, '01

"There are only hints and guesses,
hints followed by guesses, and the rest
is prayer, observance, discipline, thought and action."
— T.S. Eliot (1888-1965)

I Do Not See the Road Ahead

My Lord God, I have no idea where I am going.
I do not see the road ahead of me.
I cannot know for certain where it will end.
Nor do I really know myself,
and the fact that I think that I am following your will
does not mean that I am actually doing so.
But I believe that the desire to please you
does in fact please you.
And I hope I have that desire in all that I am doing.
I hope that I will never do anything apart from that desire.
And I know that if I do this
you will lead me by the right road
though I may know nothing about it.
Therefore will I trust you always
though I may seem to be lost
and in the shadow of death.
I will not fear, for you are ever with me,
and you will never leave me to face my perils alone.

— *Thomas Merton (1915-1968)*

God grant me the serenity
to accept the things I cannot change,
courage to change the things I can,
and the wisdom to know the difference.
Living one day at a time;
enjoying one moment at a time;
accepting hardship as the pathway to peace.
Taking, as Jesus did, this sinful world
as it is, not as I would have it;
trusting that he will make all things right
if I surrender to his will;
that I may be reasonably happy in this life
and supremely happy with Him forever in the next.

— Reinhold Niebuhr (1894-1962)

"I pray because I cannot control what is happening in my life or what is happening all around me. I pray for those that I feel need help and someone to watch over them. I pray because sometimes I feel lost in my journey of life."
— A sophomore

God, Grant Me Peace

(A Prayer in Time of Anxiety)

Gracious God, as I lie here in bed, unable to sleep because I am worrying
about the day I just had and the days I have ahead of me,
I ask for your guidance and comfort.
God, grant me peace.

Please help me to ease my mind and stop the constant analysis of
what I could have done differently and how I will do things in the future.
God, grant me peace.

Heavenly Father, remind me that I am trying my best in all that I do,
from my daily tasks to my relationships with others,
and that is all that I can ask of myself.
God, grant me peace.

Thank you, God, for my family, my friends, my work and my life.
God, grant me peace.

I am grateful for all that I have, and I know I do not always show that when I worry.
God, grant me peace.

Help me to relax, breathe and lie here calmly in your presence.
God, grant me peace

God, grant me peace.
Amen.

— Katrina D. Coakley
Director of Residential Life

"As I was with Moses, so I will be with you; I will not fail you or forsake you."
— Joshua 1:5

Prayer for a Friend in Trouble

Lord,
my friend is in trouble,
and before I even bring this problem to you in prayer,
I already feel your hand at work.
It was you who called me to my friend's side,
you who put it in my heart to pray,
you who stays with me now
while I search for the right words to say,
and you who will give me the courage to act.
Reveal yourself to me in a powerful way.
Let me be a vehicle for your Spirit,
a vessel from which your grace may flow.

Put your wisdom in my heart
and healing words in my mouth.
I can help, but I cannot do it alone.
So I pray for your Spirit
to come to me,
to guide me,
to help me be a light
bright enough
to guide a heart
back to you.
Amen.

— Anne Brucker, '04

"Come to me, all you that are weary and are carrying heavy burdens,
and I will give you rest."
— Matthew 11:28

In Difficult Times

I'm going crazy!
Lord, I'm always ready for difficulty, trouble of any kind.
Anywhere. Anytime. No matter what.
That's what I always thought.
But, now,
THIS,
this is crazy!
Things have gotten out of hand.
This is beyond me.

I need your help.

– Fr. Robert Malone, CSC
Campus Minister

"God alone is my rock and my salvation,
my fortress; I shall never be shaken."
– Psalm 62:2

For Comfort

Help me to remember
what is really important:
that I am your child
and you are my Father.
You love me for who I am and how I live,
not for what I look like or what I own.
Let me praise you who sees into my heart,
who is always with me,
and who eases my pain.
Amen.

— Author unknown

"God is with us."
— John Wesley, on his deathbed (1703-1791)

When Faith is Tested

"Faith is the assurance of things hoped for,
the conviction of things not seen."
— Hebrews 11:1.

Lord,
when a problem weighs so heavily on me
that I cannot stop thinking about it,
be with me.
When I am in pain or suffering
or have experienced sorrow,
be with me.

Strengthen me to overcome my struggles.
Help me feel hopeful for the future.
Encourage me when times are tough.
Help me find consolation and comfort in your presence.

Help me to sense your presence
in the person who sits and listens
when my heart is heavy
and needs to be poured out,
in sunshine,
in loved ones,
in laughter,
in the innocence of children,
in the beauty of nature.

Share the bad times with me
so I do not have to carry life's burdens alone.
Let me feel comfort in knowing that
you are the constant in my life,
always there, always faithful.
You will never leave me.
Your promise is for now and always.
You are my hope.
Amen.

— Janet Betts
Program Assistant, Occupational Therapy

Trust in the Lord of the Journey

(This call to patient trust, written by the Jesuit paleontologist Pierre Teilhard de Chardin, is one that we feel blessed to be able to share with our first-year students.)

Above all, trust in the slow work of God.
We are, quite naturally,
impatient in everything to reach the end
without delay.

We should like to skip
the intermediate stages.

We are impatient of being on the way to something unknown,
something new.

And yet it is
the law of all progress
that it is made by passing through stages of instability ...
and that it may take a very long time.

And so I think it is with you.
Your ideas mature gradually –
let them grow, let them shape themselves,
without undue haste.
Don't try to force them on,
as though you could be today what time
(that is to say, grace and circumstances
acting on your own good will)
will make of you tomorrow.

Only God could say what this new spirit
gradually forming within you will be.
Give our Lord the benefit of believing
that his hand is leading you,
and accept this anxiety of
feeling yourself in suspense
and incomplete.

— *Pierre Teilhard de Chardin, SJ (1881-1955)*

When I Need Healing

"I pray because I need help from God sometimes.
I need the friendship that he gives."
— Jennifer Underhill, '04

Prayer for Inner Healing

(Sit in a quiet place and allow yourself at least ten minutes to pray this prayer.)

O God, I feel like such a mess.
I look at my life and all I see are the times that I've not
been what I was supposed to be:
I've lied to save face.
I've been at the wrong place at the wrong time.
I've gotten involved with the wrong people.
I thought I loved others and realize now that
I used people to get what I wanted.
And now this —

If people really knew me, they'd want nothing to do with me.
I feel like I am a burden even to myself.
I hate feeling alone, empty and believing that no one understands or cares about me.
I think of all I've not done:
I've broken promises I've made to myself.

> I've not honored commitments I've made to others.
> I've messed up relationships, and I can't even admit that to
> the other persons.
> I've let good friends drift away
> because I thought they were unwilling or unable to love me as I wished.

I need your help, O God. I'm so scared.
Heal me of my fears, of the memories that hold me back from living fully,
and of all that restricts me from accepting my self and my life.

(Allow yourself five more minutes to hear your God say: "I have already forgiven you, my friend.")

— *Sr. Anne Louise Nadeau, SND deNamur*
Director of Personal Counseling

In Depression

O God, you care for your creation with great tenderness.
In the midst of the greatest pain, you offer hope.
Give help to me, whose spirit seems to be lost
and whose soul is in despair.
Let me feel your pure love.
Let me believe in the miracle of rebirth
so that I can experience now a small taste of the
happiness I hope to know in eternity.
Amen.

— Dimma, an Irish Monk (7th Century)

"Truly, O people in Zion, you shall weep no more.
The Lord will surely be gracious to you at the sound of your cry."
— Isaiah 30:19

Prayer to Christ the Healer

Several members of our community have told us that this prayer helped them through a time of serious illness.

In the comfort of your unfailing love,

I give over to you, my Savior,
the memories that haunt me,
the anxieties that perplex me,
the fears that stifle me,
the sickness that prevails upon me,
and the frustration of all the pain
that weaves about within me.

Lord, help me to know
your peace in my turmoil,
your compassion in my sorrow,
your forgiveness in my weakness,
and your love in my need.

Touch me, O Lord,
with your healing power and strength.
Amen.

– Alexian Brothers Health System

When Someone I Love Is Dying

Dear Father,
Today I walk alone through the valley of fear.
The world I once knew is slipping away,
and the reality I dread is closing in.
Even my memories disturb me—
things I said or should have said,
things I did or could have done
come to haunt me now.

Father, I am afraid.
Help me to trust
that all unfinished conversations
will be finished with you,
and everything left undone
will be done in paradise,
and there is no reason to fear anything at all.

Gentle God,
into your hands I commend my loved one,
into your hands I commend my sorrow.
If I have to let go—
let me remember it is only for a time,
and the one that I love
is being asked only
to come home,
to be held in your loving arms
forever and ever,
Amen.

— Campus Ministry

"Death is not a putting out of the light;
rather it is an extinguishing of the lamp
because the DAWN has come."
— Rabindranath Tagore (1861-1941)

We Seem to Give Them Back to You

We seem to give our loved ones back to you, O God,
who gave them to us.
Yet as you did not lose them in giving,
so do we not lose them by their return.
Not as the world gives, do you give, O Lover of souls.
What you give, you do not take away,
for what is yours is ours also if we are yours.

Life is eternal and love is immortal,
and death is only a horizon;
and a horizon is nothing, save the limit of our sight.
Lift us up, strong Son of God,
that we may see further;
cleanse our eyes that we may see more clearly;
draw us closer to yourself
so that we may know ourselves
to be nearer to our loved ones who are with you.

And while you are preparing a place for us,
prepare us also for that happy place,
that where you are
we may also be forevermore.
Amen.

— Bede Jarrett, OP (1881-1934)

 *"The one whom we have loved and lost
is no longer where he was before;
he is now wherever we are."*
— Saint John Chrysostom (347-407)

All shall be Amen and Alleluia.

We shall rest and we shall see;

We shall see and we shall know;

We shall know and we shall love;

We shall love and we shall praise—

Behold our end which is no end.

Amen.

– *St. Augustine of Hippo* (354-430)

"Pray without ceasing."
– I Thessalonians 5:17

The bread you do not use
is the bread of the poor.

The garment hanging in your wardrobe
is the garment of him who is naked.

The shoes you do not wear
are the shoes of one who is barefoot.

The money you keep locked away
is the money of the poor.

The acts of charity you do not perform
are so many injustices you commit.

— *Saint Basil the Great* (330-379)

"A growing engagement with the world, a willingness to encounter those who suffer from injustice, a desire to serve— these are core values of a Sacred Heart University education."
— Dr. Anthony J. Cernera, President

Over the years thousands of our students, faculty and staff members have participated in community service projects.
These prayers for justice and peace
represent our struggle as individuals and as a University
to make the world a better place.

Included in this section are prayers we use before doing volunteer work,
prayers for peace, and prayers for religious unity.
We have also included some traditional selections
that have inspired us to continue to serve others,
especially the poor.

As We Seek to Serve

Heavenly Father,
today I will serve others
as you have guided me to do.

May I be empowered by the experience.
May I empower those whom I serve.

May each one of us come away from the experience
with a deeper understanding of your will for us.

I am your servant, Lord.
Show me the way to touch the hearts of those I serve
as you have touched mine.

Amen.

— Stephanie Carvalho, '02

O Lord,
we ask that you allow us
the privilege of walking with the poor
who bring us ever closer
to your presence among us.
Help us, O Lord,
to understand that
we must learn to be silent and listen
and that we must work to earn the trust
of those whom we seek to serve.
And finally, O Lord,
we ask that you open our hearts
so we may hear the good news messages
of our brothers and sisters who,
despite suffering the ravages of our world,
teach us about hope, faith and love.
Amen.

— Dr. Ralph L. Corrigan
Professor Emeritus of English

"Without God, we cannot.
Without us, God will not."
— Saint Augustine of Hippo (354-430)

We feel fortunate that the communion of saints allows us to join our prayers with the prayers of others who have served before us, prayers that continue to inspire us now. This meditation by Cardinal Newman is one of those prayers.

God has created me to do Him some definite service;
He has committed some work to me
which He has not committed to another.
I have my mission—I may never know it in this life,
but I shall be told it in the next.

I am a link in a chain, a bond of connection between persons.
He has not created me for naught.
I shall do good, I shall do His work;
I shall be an angel of peace,
a preacher of truth in my own place, while not intending it,
if I do but keep His commandments and serve Him in my calling.

Therefore, my God, I will put myself without reserve into your hands.
What have I in heaven, and apart from you what want I upon earth?
My flesh and my heart fail,
but God is the God of my heart, and my portion forever.

— John Henry Cardinal Newman (1801-1890)

Working together for change, building community and having fun in the process are hallmarks of many of our community service programs. These programs always begin by inviting God to be a part of the work we do.

A Builder's Prayer

(Prayer for a Habitat for Humanity workday)

Dear Lord,

As we work to build a new home today, be with us and keep us safe.

Help us realize that no matter how insignificant our task may seem, every job must be done to complete a house.

Help us to use our talents to the best of our abilities—whether that talent is carpentry, organizing a group, teaching someone a new skill or approaching a difficult job with humor and a positive attitude.

Let us tear down the walls of prejudice, fear and indifference that have led to poverty and inhumane housing conditions.

Let us build not only a house, but also a community of people who can work together and care for each other despite our differences in religion, race and language.

Give us confidence that we can achieve more working together than we ever could as individuals.

Give us humility to remember that each of us has something to learn from others.

Let the work that we do this day be another step in building the kind of world you want to see—a world where people work together with their neighbors to end poverty and suffering.

Amen.

— Phyllis Machledt
Director of Service-Learning and Volunteer Programs

"The things, good Lord, that we pray for,
give us the grace to labor for."
— Saint Thomas More (1478-1535)

Mentoring programs at Sacred Heart University unite our students with children in nearby grammar schools for tutoring sessions, friendship, and individual attention. The work can be difficult, but our students will tell you that it is always rewarding.

A Mentor's Prayer

O Lord, guide me in my work
with the children I mentor.
Make me strong, patient and kind,
a consistent, persistent and respectful advocate
for the students you have entrusted to my care.
Let me be open to criticism,
willing to share what I know
and to be taught in return.
Remind me that the role of the mentor takes many forms:
listener, guide, facilitator, friend,
teacher, student, brother, sister
and one who is willing to compromise
for the sake of the child in my care.

Remind me that these children
are precious gifts from you
and that my time with them
is a chance to share
the gifts you have given to me.

Caution me to leave my own problems
at the door, allowing me to be open
to whatever each child needs from me today.

Most important, Lord,
work through me.
Let me be the vehicle
through which your love reaches
the children of Bridgeport
and all the world.
Amen

— Angela Rose Bowden, '01

"First of all, with prayer, beg that God would bring to completion every good you set out to do."
— Saint Benedict (c.480-c.547)

Many Sacred Heart University students serve as big brothers or sisters to children in Bridgeport. This prayer, by one volunteer, is for the boy who became his little brother and friend.

Prayer for Miguel

Father in heaven,
I ask you to bless
the poor, innocent children of Bridgeport.
I see them all every time I look into Miguel's eyes.
I see them because he has seen them,
because he is one of them.
This one child has been through more
than his eyes can hide or his eight years can tell.
Please God, be the father he does not have.
Watch over him, protect him, love him.
Make his life a little easier than it has been.
And guide me, Lord,
so that I may be the positive influence he needs
to grow into the kind, gentle, decent man
you created him to be.
Amen.

— Michael DiPietro, '02

We Are Christ's Body

Christ has no body now on earth but yours,
no hands but yours,
no feet but yours.
Yours are the eyes through which
Christ's compassion is to look out on the world;
Yours are the feet with which
he is to go about doing good;
Yours are the hands with which
he is to bless men and women now.

— St. Teresa of Avila (1515-1582)

"Whatever God does, the first outburst is always compassion."
— Meister Eckhart (1260-1327)

Community Connections is a program that invites first-year students to spend a week in Bridgeport in service to and with the poor. We love to share this prayer by Kate Compston with the participants because we feel it beautifully reflects the journey of self-discovery that lies at the heart of this powerful experience.

O God, Who Am I Now?

O God,
who am I now?
Once, I was secure
in familiar territory
in my sense of belonging
unquestioning of
the norms of my culture
the assumptions built into my language,
the values shared by my society.

But now you have called me out and away from home
and I do not know where you are leading.
I am empty, unsure, and uncomfortable.
I have only a beckoning star to follow.

Journeying God,
pitch your tent with mine
so that I may not become deterred
by hardship, strangeness, doubt.
Show me the movement I must make
toward a wealth not dependent on possessions
toward a wisdom not based on books
toward a strength not bolstered by might
toward a God not confined to heaven,
but scandalously earthed, poor, unrecognized...
Help me to find myself
as I walk in others' shoes.
Amen.

– Kate Compston

"Prayer is the heart's pilgrimage."
– George Herbert (1593-1633)

Curtis Week is a five-day immersion program in Bridgeport that takes place every January during winter break. It is open to students who are interested in issues of cultural diversity, racial injustice and service to the poor. The following prayer is used to send off the participants with the Sacred Heart University community's blessing.

Whom Shall We Send

O God,
our world needs healing.
Whom shall we send?

Send me, God of love,
I am ready to serve with compassion
those whom I meet this week
and see all as my sisters and brothers
regardless of their social status, race, or religion.

Our world needs understanding.
Whom shall we send?

Send me, God of wisdom,
I am ready to learn from my sisters and brothers,
from the poor, the exploited,
from those who have different ways
of seeing, living, and praying.

Our world needs witnessing.
Whom shall we send?

Send me, God of justice,
I am ready to speak out
against the injustices that I see around me
and to be a voice for those who go unheard
in their cry for freedom and human rights.

Our world is waiting.
Whom shall we send?

Send me, God of all people,
I am ready to do your work.
Amen.

— Noëlle D'Agostino
Campus Minister

"Let us develop a kind of dangerous unselfishness."
— Dr. Martin Luther King, Jr.

We are proud of the fact that, while they are at Sacred Heart University, so many of our students devote a significant amount of their time to serve the needs of others. Some of our graduates have gone on to do a postgraduate year of service with various organizations both in the United States and abroad.

This prayer was written by one of the graduates of the Class of 2001. Jeff spent a year with the Jesuit Volunteers as a support service coordinator for Casa Ita Ford in East Los Angeles.

A Volunteer's Prayer

Dear God,
as we abandon the familiar
in favor of the unknown,
watch over us.
As we leave our homes
for new opportunities to serve you,
look after the loved ones we leave behind.
Open our hearts to the suffering
of those we hope to serve.

Open our minds to the wisdom
they have to share with us.
Help us to be a source of light
to all the people that need us.
Grant us the humility of your Son,
the wisdom of your Spirit,
and the strength of your hand
as we attempt to do your will
this year, and in the years to come.
Amen.

— Jeffrey Hoose, '01

"No one has the right to sit down and feel hopeless.
There is too much work to do."
— Dorothy Day (1897-1980)

Give Me Someone

Lord Jesus,
when I am famished,
  give me someone who needs food.
When I am thirsty,
  send me someone who needs water.
When I am cold,
  send me someone to warm.
When I am hurting,
  send me someone to console.
When my cross becomes heavy,
  give me another's cross to share.
When I am poor,
  lead someone needy to me.
When I have no time,
  give me someone to help for a moment.

When I am humiliated,
  give me someone to praise.
When I am discouraged,
  send me someone to encourage.
When I need another's understanding,
  give me someone who needs mine.
When I need somebody to take care of me,
  send me someone to care for.
When I think of myself,
  turn my thoughts toward another.
And when I think I can make no difference in the lives of others,
  show me the limitless possibility
    of Christ's compassionate journey within me.

— from Japan, (Author unknown)

Each year students, faculty and staff members journey to El Salvador to learn about the country and its people. Year after year, however, the participants return to say that they have learned more about themselves than anything else. We are ever grateful to our neighbors in El Salvador whose struggle for justice continually inspires our own work and prayer. This is the prayer with which each delegation has begun its journey there.

Bless Our Journey

Lord,
wondering and amazed,
we stand before you
and ask your blessing
on the journey we are about to begin.
You, the creator of the world,
who fed the hungry
with bread and word alike,
be our inspiration now
in the work we will undertake.

Free us from the drive to seek
personal recognition for our efforts.

Help us to be strong enough
to stand with your poor,
brave enough to confront our own poverty,
weak enough to need your strength,
and wise enough to ask for help.

Demand from us that we follow
in your pattern of service,
a service that does not try to impose
your will or our own,
but works
and waits
for your kingdom
to come.
Amen.

— Campus Ministry

"In the last analysis, what does the word 'sacrifice' mean? Or even the word 'gift'?
One who has nothing can give nothing. The gift is God's—to God."
— Dag Hammarskjöld (1905-1961)

Although not formally a "prayer," this poem reflects the heart of the service experience in El Salvador.

The Moon Was Full

The moon was full last night
and God said to me, "Go
forward and use me as
your guiding light. And
if you lose your way
just look up and I'll be there."

The moon was full last night
and God said to me, "Go
and do not be afraid. You
are doing my will and
I will guide you. I told
the moon to shine all
night long, so if you
lose your way, just look up."

   The moon was full last night
and I was scared. I said to myself,
"What have you gotten yourself into?"
I was losing my way, and
I looked up. And in the
moon's light, God comforted me.

The moon was full last night
and my Lord guided me.
He helped me rejoice in the fact
that I was taking an active part in life.
He calmed my fears
and strengthened my faith in him.
He said, "Go and learn and see the
truth you've been searching for."

The moon was full last night and I smiled.

— Angela Paulone, '01

As We Dare to Dream

A better world—one where the lion lies down with the lamb, and compassion and tolerance reign—is the dream of many Sacred Heart University students. This prayer by a senior touched our hearts.

A Time for Prayer

I pray for a time when we all shall embrace
the teachings of compassion and the philosophy of grace.

I pray for a century when we are all gentle and kind,
a span of collected moments in which we all are color blind.

I pray for a decade when we are not at war
over religious beliefs and cultural differences,
and we authentically ask the question: what are we fighting for?

I pray for a year when tragedy does not strike,
neither by the ugliness of human hand nor by nature's might.

I pray for a month when not one child
goes hungry, nor dies from starvation.

I pray for a week when we all shall grow strong
on the journey toward right in our triumphant battle over wrong.

I pray for the day when we all shall value and uphold
the teaching of Mahatma Gándhi and Jesus, more than we do
earthly treasures such as diamonds and gold.

I pray for the hour when we all shall decree our mission
is to love without fear, measure, labels, shame, an end, or condition.

I pray for the minute when we all shall gain a true innerstanding
that life is a beautiful and enjoyable flight,
but at times may also include an emergency landing.

I pray for the second when we all shall
feel his touch and in his peace find rest,
knowing his love for you and me is as immeasurable
as the distance held between the east and the west.

I pray for a time when we all shall embrace
the teachings of compassion and the philosophy of grace.

– Brandon M. Graham, '02

For All God's People

God of wisdom,
create in us a spirit of understanding
so that we may learn from one another in our rich faith traditions,
different ways of seeing, living, and praying.

God of love,
create in us a spirit of compassion
so that we may reach out to those in need in our community
and in our world.

God of mercy,
create in us a spirit of forgiveness,
so that we may begin to heal the wounds that we have borne
and that we have inflicted.

God of truth,
create in us a spirit of justice,
so that together as a people we may be open in mind and heart
to answer the call to witness and to action,
to be a voice for those who have none.

God of all people,
be born in our hearts today and every day,
so that we may be a light of peace and hope to our broken world.

– Noëlle D'Agostina
Campus Minister

"Prayer does not change God, but changes the one who prays."
– Søren Kierkegaard (1813-1855)

For Unity Among Peoples of Different Faiths

Almighty God,
grant us the wisdom and humility to acknowledge you as
the Creator and supreme power of the Universe.

You have fashioned us in your image.
You have breathed life into us and into all living things.
Give us the strength to be a source of goodness and kindness
for all that you have brought into existence.

It is your will that we should be many peoples and cultures.
Unite all your children in the desire to do your will.
May each one of us contribute to the best of our ability
to making this a better world for all humanity.

May peace of mind, peace of spirit
and world peace reign soon.

Amen.

— Rabbi Joseph Ehrenkranz
Executive Director
The Center for Christian-Jewish Understanding

Although we do not know its origin, this prayer is one we use often to initiate group discussions on peace and justice issues. It challenges us to dream big and to work hard to build a better world.

Disturb Us, Lord

Disturb us, Lord, when we are too well-pleased with ourselves,
when our dreams have come true because we shall have dreamed too little,
when we arrived safely because we sailed too close to the shore.

Disturb us, Lord, when, with the abundance of the things we possess,
we have lost our thirst for the water of life.

Stir us, Lord, to dare more boldly, to venture on wilder seas
where storms will show your majesty;
where, losing sight of land, we shall find the stars.

We ask you to push us in strength, courage, hope and love.

Amen.

— *Author unknown*

Teach Me To Stand Up Free

God, give me the courage to be
revolutionary
as your Son Jesus Christ was.
Give me the courage to loosen myself
from this world.
Teach me to stand up free
and to shun no criticism.
God, it is for your kingdom.
Make me free,
make me poor in this world.
Then will I be rich in the real world,
which this life is all about.
God, thank you for the vision of the future,
but make it fact and not just theory.

— Henri Nouwen (1932-1996)

"I pray because I am incomplete without my Lord, and without Him I am nothing. I pray
because He has given me so much that I want to thank Him and make Him proud."
— Christopher Barr, '04

For a Just World

Dear God,
it is up to us to help the world in any way we can.
This is why you have put us here.
This is why you have put me here, but I need your help.
I cannot do anything alone.
It will take a great deal of love and compassion to make a more just world.
Remind me that you are with me in this struggle.
Help me to see that the little changes I can effect today
will become the seeds of bigger changes that I hope will come tomorrow.
And little changes are a good starting place for someone like me
who wants to make a difference in this world.
Amen.

— Lori Coupe, '04

"Faith without works is dead."
— James 1:22

"You must be the change you wish to see in the world."
— Mahatma Gandhi (1869-1948)

Dear Lord,

Grant me appreciation of the journey,
for peace and justice are ever redefining themselves.

Enhance my ability to see my reflection in other people's faces,
for this is my traveling suit.

Fuel my passage with raw honesty, commitment, tolerance and the ability to
cry and console, so to propel me down the twisted road from retribution to
reconciliation.

Prepare me to accept differences and complexities, to transform perceptions
of complicity to perceptions of connectedness.

Dear Lord, please light up my path and empower me to be part of dignifying
the lives of my brothers and sisters.

— Gloria Rosa-Wendelboe
Administrative Secretary
Office of Service-Learning and Volunteer Programs

The following prayer was often quoted by Mother Teresa of Calcutta (1910-1997).

Universal Prayer for Peace

Lead me from death to life,
from falsehood to truth.
Lead me from despair to hope,
from fear to trust.
Lead me from hate to love,
from war to peace.
Let peace fill our heart, our world, our universe.
Peace, peace, peace.

— Adapted from the Upanishads by Satish Kumar

"For Christ is our peace; in his flesh he has made both groups into one and has broken down the dividing wall that is the hostility between us."

— Ephesians 2:14

"And what does the Lord require of you
but to do justice, and to love kindness,
and to walk humbly with your God?"
— *Micah 6:8*

Whenever we are tempted to get discouraged, we are inspired by the prophetic life and heroic martyrdom of Oscar Romero, Archbishop of San Salvador. His powerful words give us strength as we dare to dream.

It helps, now and then,
to step back and take the long view.
The Kingdom is not only beyond our efforts,
it is even beyond our vision.
We accomplish in our lifetime only a tiny fraction
of the magnificent enterprise that is God's work.
Nothing we do is complete,
which is another way of saying that
the Kingdom always lies beyond us.

No statement says all that should be said.
No prayer fully expresses our faith.
No confession brings perfection.
No pastoral visit brings wholeness.
No program accomplishes the church's mission.
No set of goals and objectives includes everything.

This is what we are about.
We plant the seeds that one day will grow.
We water seeds already planted,
knowing that they hold future promise.
We lay foundations
that will need further development.
We provide yeast
that produces effects far beyond our capabilities.

We cannot do everything, and there is
a sense of liberation in realizing that.
This enables us to do something,
and to do it very well.
It may incomplete, but it is a beginning,
a step along the way,
an opportunity for the Lord's grace
to enter and do the rest.

We may never see the end results,
but that is the difference
between the master builder and the worker.

We are workers, not master builders,
ministers, not messiahs.

We are prophets of a future that is not our own.

— *Oscar A. Romero (1917-1980)*

Prayer is naught else
but a yearning of soul...
when it is practiced
with the whole heart,
it has great power.

— *Saint Mechthild of Magdeburg (1210-c.1280)*

V. Prayers that endure the test of time

Here is a small sampling from the vast treasury of traditional Catholic prayers as well as some others that have stood the test of time. Some of these traditional prayers will be familiar to you, others may not.

Read them.

Pray them.

Live them.

They are the Church's time-honored, Spirit-inspired gift to us.

Let them speak to and for your heart.

Sign of the Cross

This prayer serves as the beginning and conclusion of every prayer and action. It is said while one uses the right hand to trace the shape of a cross over one's forehead, heart and shoulders. By this prayer, we sanctify our lives in consecration to the three Persons of the Blessed Trinity.

In the name of the Father,
and of the Son, and of the Holy Spirit.
Amen.

Our Father

Jesus gave this prayer to his disciples when they asked Him to teach them how to pray (Matthew 6:9-13). For this reason, it is the model for all Christian prayer.

Our Father, who art in heaven, hallowed be thy name;
thy kingdom come, thy will be done
on earth as it is in heaven.
Give us this day our daily bread;
and forgive us our trespasses
as we forgive those who trespass against us;
and lead us not into temptation,
but deliver us from evil.
Amen.

"Whenever you pray, go into your room and shut the door and pray to your Father who is in secret; and your Father who sees in secret will reward you. ... For your Father knows what you need before you ask Him."
— Matthew 6:6,8

Hail Mary

This prayer is based on a passage from the Gospel of Luke, which contains the first line of the prayer (Luke 1: 28). By the beginning of the twelfth century, the first part of the prayer was in common use in the liturgy of the West. The second part of the prayer (beginning, "Holy Mary") was added officially during the sixteenth century.

Hail Mary, full of grace!
The Lord is with you;
blessed are you among women,
and blessed is the fruit of your womb, Jesus.
Holy Mary, Mother of God,
pray for us sinners, now
and at the hour of our death.
Amen.

"Prayer is a surge of the heart, a cry of recognition and love embracing both trial and joy."
— Saint Thérèse of Lisieux (1873-1897)

Glory Be

(The Doxology)

A profession in praise of the Blessed Trinity,
this prayer has been in use since the early days of the Church.

Glory be to the Father, and to the Son,
and to the Holy Spirit. As it was in the
beginning, is now, and will be forever.

Amen.

"Prayer is the mortar that holds our house together."
— Saint Teresa of Avila (1515-1282)

Apostles' Creed

This prayer is an ancient creed used at baptisms in the early Church.
It is a summary of the teaching of the apostles.

I believe in God, the Father almighty, creator of heaven and earth.
I believe in Jesus Christ, his only Son, our Lord.
He was conceived by the power of the Holy Spirit and born of the Virgin Mary.
He suffered under Pontius Pilate, was crucified, died, and was buried.
He descended into hell. On the third day he rose again.
He ascended into heaven and is seated at the right hand of the Father.
He will come again to judge the living and the dead.
I believe in the Holy Spirit, the holy Catholic Church,
the communion of saints, the forgiveness of sins,
the resurrection of the body, and life everlasting.
Amen.

"I pray because I believe in Christ. I pray because I feel I need to."
— Jason Healy, '05

Act of Faith

O my God, I firmly believe that you are one God
in three divine Persons, Father, Son, and Holy Spirit;
I believe that your divine Son became human and died for our sins
and that he will come to judge the living and the dead.
I believe these and all the truths
that the holy Catholic Church teaches,
because you have revealed them,
who can neither deceive nor be deceived.
Amen.

Act of Hope

O my God, relying on your almighty power
and infinite mercy and promises,
I hope to obtain pardon for my sins,
the help of your grace,
and life everlasting,
through the merits of Jesus Christ,
my Lord and Redeemer.
Amen.

Act of Love

O my God, I love you above all things,
with my whole heart and soul,
because you are all good and worthy of all love.
I love my neighbor as myself for the love of you.
I forgive all who have injured me
and ask pardon of all whom I have injured.

Amen.

"I pray because my life depends on it."
– Dr. Donna Dodge, SC
Vice President for Mission and Planning

Act of Contrition

O my God, I am heartily sorry for all my sins. In choosing to do wrong and failing to do good, I have sinned against you whom I should love above all things. I firmly intend, with your help, to do penance, to sin no more, and to avoid whatever leads me to sin. Our Savior Jesus Christ suffered and died for us. In his name, my God, have mercy. Amen.

"I pray because it releases all the negative energy I have built up in me. When I tell God all that is bothering me, I feel somehow clean. And sometimes, if you listen very closely, you can get some answers or some reassurance from God."
— Deborah Dietzel, '03

"It is not what you are

nor what you have been

that God sees with all-merciful eyes,

but what you desire to be."

– from The Cloud of Unknowing (Fourteenth century)

Hail, Holy Queen

Hail, holy Queen, mother of mercy,

hail, our life, our sweetness, and our hope.

To you we cry, poor banished children of Eve;

to you we send up our sighs,

mourning and weeping in this valley of tears.

Turn then, most gracious advocate,

your eyes of mercy toward us,

and after this our exile,

show unto us the blessed fruit of your womb, Jesus.

O clement, O loving, O sweet virgin Mary.

"Let the soul of Mary be in each one of you to magnify the Lord.
Let the spirit of Mary be in each one to exult in God."
— Saint Ambrose, Bishop of Milan (339-397)

The Memorare

Remember, O most gracious Virgin Mary,
 that never was it known
  that anyone who fled to your protection,
   implored your help,
    or sought your intercession
     was left unaided.
Inspired with this confidence,
 I fly unto you,
  O Virgin of virgins, my Mother.
   To you do I come, before you I stand,
    sinful and sorrowful.
O Mother of the Word incarnate,
 despise not my petitions,
  but in your mercy
   hear and answer me.
Amen.

Prayers to My Guardian Angel

My Guardian Angel,
God has sent you to me to guide me;
I am in your care.
Be my constant companion
and protect me throughout this day.
Do not let me go astray
and warn me of every danger
to both body and soul.
Amen.

"I pray because without prayer I feel alone."
— Baida Al-Ayyar, '02

Angel of God, my guardian dear,
to whom God's love commits me here,
ever this day be at my side,
to light and guard, to rule and guide.
Amen.

This ancient communion prayer is taken from The Didache ("The Teaching"), a short manual on morals and Church practice, written in the second century.

Now concerning the Eucharistic meal,
give thanks in this manner.

First, concerning the cup:
we thank you, our Father,
for the holy vine of David your servant,
whom you made known to us through your servant Jesus;
may the glory be yours forever.

Concerning the broken bread:
we thank you, our Father,
for the life and knowledge
which you made known to us through your servant Jesus;
may the glory be yours forever.

As this broken bread was scattered over the mountains
and was gathered together to become one,
so let your Church be gathered together
from the ends of the earth into your kingdom;
for the glory and power are yours
through Jesus Christ forever.
Amen.

Grace before Meals

Bless us, O Lord, and these your gifts,
which we are about to receive from your bounty,
through Christ our Lord. Amen.

Blessed are you, Father, who gives us our daily bread.
Blessed is your only begotten Son, who continually
feeds us with the word of life.
Blessed is the Holy Spirit, who brings us
together at this table of love.
Blessed be God now and forever. Amen.

Grace after Meals

We thank you, O Lord,
for these gifts and for all the gifts
we have received from your goodness,
through Christ our Lord. Amen.

O God, you provide for every living thing.
Thank you for the food we have just enjoyed.
Give us hearts that will reach out to the poor.
May we share your gifts of food and material blessings
with those who do not have what we have
so that one day we may sit down together with them
at the heavenly banquet table.
We ask this through Christ our Lord. Amen.

Prayer Before Study

Lord, my God, direct my study,
ensure my perseverance,
and set your seal upon its completion.
You who are the fount of wisdom,
shed light upon the darkness of my understanding
and dispel the twofold darkness of sin and ignorance.
Grant me a keen understanding, a retentive memory,
method and ease in learning, fluency in speech and writing.
Finally, set me on a way of life that is pleasing to you
and grant me confidence that I will embrace you at the end.
Amen.

— Saint Thomas Aquinas (1225-1274)
Patron Saint of Catholic Universities

"I pray because I want to discover as much about God's plan for me here on earth as I possibly can. I pray because I have faith in the words of devotion and their impact. I believe my words really do reach the ears of God and that he will always be receptive to what I have to say, even if the outside world does not listen. I pray because I trust in God and his will, and if I am apprehensive, I find meaning and peace in the ritual of prayer. I believe that the fervor of the heart in prayer can accomplish more than mere activities."

— Cristina Baptista, '05

To Christ, Our Only Teacher

Thank you, Jesus, for bringing me this far.
In your light, I see the light of my life.
Your teaching is brief and to the point:
you persuade us to trust in our heavenly Father;
you command us to love one another.
What is easier than to believe in God?
What is sweeter than to love Him?
Your yoke is pleasant, your burden is light,
you, the only teacher.
You promise everything to those who obey your teaching;
you ask nothing too hard for a believer,
nothing a lover can refuse.
Your promises to your disciples are true,
entirely true, nothing but the truth.
Even more, you promise us yourself,
the perfection of all that can be made perfect.
Thank you, Jesus, now and always.
Amen.

— *Nicholas of Cusa (1401-1464)*

Let Nothing Disturb You

Let nothing disturb you,
nothing affright you;
All things are passing,
God never changes.
Patience attains
all that it strives for;
Who possesses God
finds nothing lacking:
God alone suffices.

— *Saint Teresa of Avila (1515-1582)*

*"Do not worry about anything,
but in everything by prayer and supplication with thanksgiving
let your requests be made known to God.
And the peace of God, which surpasses all understanding,
will guard your hearts and your minds in Christ Jesus."*
— *Philippians 4:6-7*

Prayer of Saint Francis

Lord, make me an instrument of your peace.
Where there is hatred, let me sow love.
Where there is injury, pardon.
Where there is doubt, faith.
Where there is despair, hope.
Where there is darkness, light.
Where there is sadness, joy.

O Divine Master, grant that I may not so much seek
to be consoled, as to console;
to be understood, as to understand;
to be loved, as to love;
for it is in giving that we receive,
it is in pardoning that we are pardoned.
and it is in dying that we are born to eternal life.

– Saint Francis of Assisi (1181-1226)

"I pray because it is the most personal and fulfilling expression of my faith. It helps me to be aware of who and where I am. When I am in need of comfort, it reminds me that I am unconditionally loved. When I am in need of guidance, it helps me to be grateful. I always feel better for praying and some- times the good feeling is powerful. I pray because I am a better person for doing it."
– Dr. Edward W. Malin
Associate Professor of Psychology

Christ Everywhere

May the strength of God guide me this day,
and may God's power preserve me.
    May the wisdom of God instruct me:
    the eye of God watch over me;
    the ear of God hear me;
    the word of God give sweetness to my speech;
    the hand of God defend me;
    and may I follow the way of God.
        Christ be with me, Christ before me,
        Christ be after me, Christ within me,
        Christ beneath me, Christ above me,
        Christ at my right hand, Christ at my left.
        Christ where I lie, Christ where I sit, Christ where I rise.
        Christ in the heart of everyone who thinks of me,
        Christ in the mouth of everyone who speaks to me,
        Christ in every eye that sees me,
        Christ in every ear that hears me.

*– Said to be on the breastplate of
Saint Patrick, Bishop of Ireland (390-460)*

174

What is more pleasing than a psalm?
David expressed it well:

> *"Praise the Lord, for a psalm is good:*
> *let there be praise of our God*
> *with gladness and grace!"*
>
> *Yes, a psalm is*
> > *a blessing on the lips of the people,*
> > *praise of God,*
> > *the assembly's homage,*
> > *a general acclamation,*
> > *a word that speaks for all,*
> > *the voice of the Church,*
> > *a confession of faith in song.*

— St. Ambrose of Milan *(339-397)*

The Prayers of Jesus

The renowned spiritual guide Henri Nouwen was once asked what advice he would give to someone who was seeking a spiritual life. Without hesitation Nouwen replied that the best way to find a spiritual life is to spend at least a year living with a group of people who pray the Psalms together every day. The Psalms—the prayers that Jesus himself prayed.

The Psalms of King David and the various canticles from the Hebrew Scriptures have formed the traditional vocabulary and rhythm of prayer for faithful Jews since long before the time of Jesus. The Church has continued to preserve this rich tradition in the pattern of daily prayer that we know as the Liturgy of the Hours, using the Psalms as well as canticles and readings from both the Hebrew Scriptures and the New Testament. When we pray Morning Prayer, Evening Prayer, or Night Prayer, we unite ourselves to the common prayer of believers around the world.

In the pages that follow, you will find a few of our favorite psalms as well as a Morning Prayer, an Evening Prayer, and a Night Prayer that we invite you to pray together with friends, family, roommates, or colleagues.

Psalm 23

The Lord is my shepherd, I shall not want.
  He makes me lie down in green pastures;
he leads me beside still waters;
  he restores my soul.
He leads me in right paths
  for his name's sake.

Even though I walk through the darkest valley,
  I fear no evil:
for you are with me;
  your rod and your staff—
  they comfort me.

You prepare a table before me
  in the presence of my enemies;
you anoint my head with oil;
  my cup overflows.
Surely goodness and mercy shall follow me
  all the days of my life
and I shall dwell in the house of the Lord
  my whole life long.

Psalm 145:1-3, 8-11, 14-18

I will extol you, my God and King,
    and bless your name for ever and ever.
Every day I will bless you
    and praise your name for ever and ever.
Great is the Lord and greatly to be praised;
    there is no end to his greatness.

        The Lord is gracious and merciful,
            slow to anger and abounding in steadfast love.
        The Lord is good to all,
            and his compassion is over all that he has made.

All your works shall give thanks to you, O Lord,
    and all your faithful shall bless you.
They shall speak of the glory of your kingdom,
    and tell of your power;

The Lord is faithful in all his words,
and gracious in all his deeds.
The Lord upholds all who are falling;
and raises up all who are bowed down.

The eyes of all look to you,
and you give them their food in due season.
You open your hand,
satisfying the desire of every living thing.

The Lord is just in all his ways
and kind in all his doings.
The Lord is near to all who call on him,
to all who call on him in truth.

Psalm 46

God is our refuge and strength,
    a very present help in trouble.
Therefore we will not fear, though the earth should change,
    though the mountains shake in the heart of the sea:
though its waters roar and foam,
    though the mountains tremble with its tumult.

                    There is a river whose streams make glad the city of God,
                        the holy habitation of the Most High.
                    God is in the midst of the city; it shall not be moved;
                        God will help it when the morning dawns.

The nations are in an uproar, the kingdoms totter;
    he utters his voice, the earth melts.
The Lord of hosts is with us;
    the God of Jacob is our refuge.

                    Come behold the works of the Lord;
                        see what desolations he has brought on the earth.
                    He makes wars cease to the end of the earth;
                        he breaks the bow, and shatters the spear;
                        he burns the shields with fire.

"Be still, and know that I am God!
    I am exalted among the nations,
    I am exalted in the earth."
The Lord of hosts is with us;
    the God of Jacob is our refuge.

Morning Prayer

Remembering God's presence

The following verse (or an appropriate song or poem) may be used to help us to place ourselves in the presence of God.

Come into my soul, O God, as the dawn breaks into the sky;
— **let your sun rise in my heart at the coming of day.**

Singing psalms to God

One or both of the following psalms (or another appropriate psalm) may be recited.

Psalm 121:1-8

I lift up my eyes to the hills—
    from where will my help come?
My help comes from the Lord,
    who made heaven and earth.

He will not let your foot be moved;
    he who keeps you will not slumber.
He who keeps Israel
    will neither slumber nor sleep.

The Lord is your keeper;
	the Lord is your shade at your right hand.
The sun shall not strike you by day,
	nor the moon by night.

The Lord will keep you from all evil;
	he will keep your life.
The Lord will keep
	your going out and your coming in
	from this time on and forevermore.

Glory to the Father and to the Son
	and to the Holy Spirit,
As it was in the beginning, is now,
	and will be forever. Amen.

Psalm 27: 1, 4-5, 8, 13-14

The Lord is my light and my salvation;
	whom shall I fear?
The Lord is the stronghold of my life;
	of whom shall I be afraid?

One thing I ask of the Lord, that I will seek after;
to live in the house of the Lord
all the days of my life;
to behold the beauty of the Lord,
and to inquire in his temple.
For he will hide me in his shelter
in the day of trouble;
he will conceal me under the cover of his tent;
he will set me high on a rock.
Hear, O Lord, when I cry aloud,
be gracious to me and answer me!
"Come," my heart says, "seek his face!"
Your face, Lord, do I seek.
Do not hide your face from me.
I believe that I shall see the goodness of the Lord
in the land of the living.
Wait for the Lord;
be strong, and let your heart take courage;
wait for the Lord!
Glory to the Father and to the Son
and to the Holy Spirit,
As it was in the beginning, is now,
and will be forever. Amen.

Listening to God's Word: Colossians 3:12-15

(or another passage from Scripture)

As God's chosen ones, holy and beloved, clothe yourselves with compassion, kindness, humility, meekness, and patience. Bear with one another and, if anyone has a complaint against another, forgive each other; just as the Lord has forgiven you, so you also must forgive. Above all, clothe yourselves with love, which binds everything together in perfect harmony. And let the peace of Christ rule in your hearts, to which indeed you were called in the one body. And be thankful.

Responding to God's Word

Glory be to God
— **whose power working in us can do immeasurably more than we can ask or imagine.**

— Ephesians 3:20,

(Note: the response may also take the form of silence, a shared reflection, a poem, music, or a song.)

Praising God: Canticle of Zechariah

Blessed be the Lord, the God of Israel,
for he has come to his people and set them free.

He has raised up a mighty savior for us,
born of the house of his servant David.
as he had promised through his holy prophets of old
that he would save us from our enemies,
from the hands of all who hate us.

He has shown mercy to our ancestors
and has remembered his holy covenant,
the oath he swore to our ancestor Abraham:
to set us free from the hands of our enemies,
so that we might worship him without fear,
holy and righteous in his sight
all the days of our life.

And you, my child, shall be called the prophet of the Most High;
for you will go before the Lord to prepare his way,
giving his people knowledge of salvation
by the forgiveness of their sins.

In the tender compassion of our God
the dawn from on high shall break upon us,
to give light to those who dwell in darkness and the shadow of death,
and to guide our feet into the way of peace.

Glory be to the Father, and to the Son,
and to the Holy Spirit.
As it was in the beginning, is now,
and will be forever. Amen.

– adapted from Luke 1:68-79

Bringing our needs to God

Jesus, you promised to be with us always, even to the end of time.
— **Please be with us now as we begin this day.**

When we face circumstances that challenge or frighten us,
— **remind us to seek your help as the day unfolds.**

When we are confused and uncertain,
— **give us patience and trust.**

When pain or worry overwhelms those we love,
— **hear the cries of our hearts.**

When we find ourselves tempted,
— **may we hold fast to you.**

When we are threatened by evil,
— **enkindle good within us.**

And for the greatest cares of this day,
— **we turn now to you.**

(Add your own petitions here.)

Our Father...

Asking God's blessing as we go forth

Grant, Lord, to all of us who study or teach,
the grace to love that which is worth loving,
to know that which is worth knowing,
to value what is most precious to you,
and to reject whatever is evil in your eyes.
Give us a true sense of judgment,
and the wisdom to see beneath the surface of things.
Above all, may we search out and do
what is pleasing to you,
through Jesus Christ our Lord. Amen.

— adapted from a prayer by Thomas à Kempis (1380-1471)

Lord, bless us and keep us.
Lord, make your face to shine upon us and be gracious to us.
Lord, lift up the light of your countenance upon us
and give us peace, now and always. Amen.

— adapted from Numbers 6:24-26

Evening Prayer

Remembering God's presence

The following verse (or an appropriate song or poem) may be used to help us to place ourselves in the presence of God.

It is you, O God, who light my lamp
—**You alone, O God, make my darkness to be light.**

Singing psalms to God

One or both of the following psalms (or another appropriate psalm) may be recited.

Psalm 62:1-2,5-6,7-8

For God alone my soul waits in silence;
    from him comes my salvation.
He alone is my rock and my salvation, my fortress;
    I shall never be shaken.

On God rests my deliverance and my honor;
    my mighty rock, my refuge is in God.
Trust in him at all times, O people;
    pour out your heart before him;
      God is a refuge for us.

Those of low estate are but a breath,
    those of high estate are a delusion;
in the balances they go up;
    they are together lighter than a breath.

Put no confidence in extortion,
    and set no vain hopes on robbery;
if riches increase,
    do not set your heart on them.

Once God has spoken;
    twice have I heard this:
that power belongs to God,
    and steadfast love belongs to you, O Lord.
For you repay to all
    according to their work.

Glory to the Father and to the Son
    and to the Holy Spirit,
As it was in the beginning, is now,
    and will be forever. Amen.

Psalm 130:1-6a,7-8

Out of the depths I cry to you, O Lord.
    Lord, hear my voice!
Let your ears be attentive
    to the voice of my supplications!

If you, O Lord, should mark iniquities,
    Lord, who could stand?
But there is forgiveness with you,
    so that you may be revered.

I wait for the Lord, my soul waits,
    and in his word I hope;
my soul waits for the Lord
    more than those who watch for the morning,

O Israel, hope in the Lord!
    For with the Lord there is steadfast love,
    and with him is great power to redeem.
It is he who will redeem Israel
    from all its iniquities.

Glory to the Father and to the Son
    and to the Holy Spirit,
As it was in the beginning, is now,
    and will be forever. Amen.

Listening to God's Word: Thessalonians 5:14-18

(or another passage from Scripture)

And we urge you, beloved, to admonish the idlers, encourage the fainthearted, help the weak, be patient with all of them. See that none of you repays evil for evil, but always seek to do good to one another and to all. Rejoice always, pray without ceasing, give thanks in all circumstances; for this is the will of God in Christ Jesus for you.

Responding to God's Word

God is not far from each one of us.
—For in him we live and move and have our being.
                              – Acts 17:28

(Note: the response may also take the form of silence, a shared reflection, a poem, music, or a song.)

Praising God: Canticle of Mary

My soul proclaims the greatness of the Lord,
my spirit rejoices in God my Savior;
for he has looked with favor on the lowliness of his servant.

From this day all generations will call me blessed;
for the Almighty has done great things for me,
and holy is his name.

He has mercy on those who fear him
from generation to generation.
He has shown the strength of his arm,
he has scattered the proud in their conceit.

He has brought down the mighty from their thrones
and has lifted up the lowly.

He has filled the hungry with good things
and has sent the rich away empty.

He has come to the help of his servant Israel
in remembrance of his promise of mercy,
the promise he made to our ancestors,
to Abraham and his descendants forever.

Glory be to the Father, and to the Son,
and to the Holy Spirit.
As it was in the beginning, is now,
and will be forever. Amen.

– adapted from Luke 1:46-55

Bringing our needs to God

For the peace of the world,
— that a spirit of respect and forbearance may grow among nations and peoples.

For the holy church of God,
— that it may be filled with truth and love and be found without fault at the day of your coming.

For those in positions of public trust, (especially …),
— that they may serve justice and promote the dignity and freedom of all people.

For a blessing upon the labors of all,
— that we may exercise the right use of the riches of creation.

For the poor, the persecuted, the sick, and all who suffer, for refugees, prisoners, and all who are in danger,
— that they may be relieved and protected.

For this community, for those who are present and for those who are absent,
—that we may be delivered from hardness of heart and show forth your glory in all that we do.

(Add your own petitions here.)

For all who have died in the faith of Christ, that, with all the saints,
— they may have rest in that place where there is no pain or grief, but life eternal.

— adapted from an ancient Byzantine litany

Our Father . . .

Asking God's blessing as we go forth

O gracious and holy Father,
give us wisdom to perceive you,
intelligence to understand you,
diligence to seek you,
patience to wait for you,
eyes to behold you,
a heart to meditate upon you,
and a life to proclaim you,
through the power of the Spirit
of our Lord Jesus Christ. Amen.

— Saint Benedict (c.480-c.547)

Lord, bless us and keep us.
Lord, make your face to shine upon us and be gracious to us.
Lord, lift up the light of your countenance upon us
    and give us peace, now and always. Amen.

— adapted from Numbers 6:24-26

Night Prayer

Remembering God's presence

The following verse (or an appropriate song or poem) may be used to help us to place ourselves in the presence of God.

> Day is done.
> Gone the sun
> From the lake,
> From the hills,
> From the sky.
> All is well,
> Safely rest:
> God is nigh.
> — *Taps*

Looking back on the day—with God's eyes

It is traditional to spend a few minutes in silent reflection to examine one's conscience. Here are a few questions:

- Do I love God with my whole heart, soul and mind?
- Did my actions today reflect this love?
- Was there a 'Sabbath' in my day, a special time reserved just for God?
- Did I make choices that showed a respect for my mind, body and spirit?
- Was I truthful and honest in all that I said and did?
- Could others have identified me as a Christian if they observed my speech, actions and attitudes? If not, am I willing to try harder tomorrow to live the way God wants me to?

Singing psalms to God

The following psalm (or another appropriate psalm) may be recited.

Psalm 91

You who live in the shelter of the Most High,
    who abide in the shadow of the Almighty,
will say to the Lord, "My refuge and my fortress;
    my God, in whom I trust."

You will not fear the terror of the night,
    or the arrow that flies by day,
or the pestilence that stalks in darkness,
    or the destruction that wastes at noonday.
A thousand may fall at your side,
    ten thousand at your right hand,
    but it will not come near you.

Because you have made the Lord your refuge,
    the Most High your dwelling place,
no evil shall befall you,
    no scourge come near your tent.
For he will command his angels concerning you
    to guard you in all your ways.

Those who love me, I will deliver;
    I will protect those who know my name.
When they call to me, I will answer them;
    I will be with them in trouble,
    I will rescue them and honor them.
With long life I will satisfy them,
    and show them my salvation.

Glory to the Father and to the Son
    and to the Holy Spirit,
As it was in the beginning, is now,
    and will be forever. Amen.

Listening to God's Word: Lamentations 3:22-24

(or another passage from Scripture)

The favors of the Lord are not exhausted,
his mercies are not spent;
They are renewed each morning,
so great is his faithfulness.
My portion is the Lord, says my soul;
therefore I will hope in him.

Responding to God's Word

You have created us and directed us towards yourself, O Lord,
— and our hearts are restless, until they rest in you.

— Saint Augustine of Hippo (354-430)

(Note: the response may also take the form of silence, a shared reflection, a poem, music, or a song.)

Praising God: Canticle of Simeon

At last, O Master, you give leave to your servant,
   to go in peace according to your promise;
for my eyes have seen your salvation,
   which you have prepared in the sight of the nations,
a light of revelation for the Gentiles,
   and glory for your people Israel.

Glory be to the Father, and to the Son,
   and to the Holy Spirit.
As it was in the beginning, is now,
   and will be forever. Amen.

— adapted from Luke 2:29-32

Asking God's blessing as we end our day

> O God,
> in this quiet moment, help us to know
> that tonight there is no need to fear
> because we are in your hands.
> Whatever awaits us tomorrow,
> we can cope with then.
> Amen.

Lord, bless us and keep us.
Lord, make your face to shine upon us and be gracious to us.
Lord, lift up the light of your countenance upon us
    and give us peace, now and always. Amen.
– adapted from Numbers 6:24-26

My brothers and sisters, let us close on a quiet note,

so that God's gentle yet powerful word of grace within us

is not drowned by our loud weak human words.

Let us pray: "Lord, help my unbelief,"

give me the grace of faith in Jesus Christ our Lord,

in his gospel and his saving power.

– Karl Rahner, S.J. (1904-1984)

Special Acknowledgements

Without the help of the following persons, this volume would not have been possible. Thank you to:

> Dr. Anthony J. Cernera, for his vision and leadership.
> Ms. Roberta Reynolds, for her creativity and patience.
> Dr. Sid Gottlieb, for his advice and encouragement.
> Ms. Michelle Quinn and Dr. David Coppola, Ph.D., for their assistance in editing.
> Ms. Carol-Anne Dabek and Ms. Jennifer Momplaisir, for their generous help.
> Dr. Donna Dodge, SC, for her support and encouragement.

> A special "thank you" to the Campus Ministry staff whose work inspires many of us to pray and whose gentle persuading moved many pray-ers to contribute to this collection.

We are grateful to the authors and publishers who have given permission to include material copyrighted or controlled by them. Every effort has been made to determine the ownership of all the texts and to make proper arrangements for their use. If any required acknowledgments have been omitted or any rights overlooked, it is unintentional. If notified, the publishers will be pleased to correct any omission in future editions. Names of prayers refer to titles used by the editor for this collection. This section constitutes a continuation of the copyright page.

Acknowledgement is made to the following, in order of appearance, for permission to reprint material from the books listed below:

"Be not forgetful of prayer" by Fyodor M. Dostoyevsky, from *The Brothers Karamazov,* translated by Constance Black Garnett ©1943, Random House, Inc. All rights reserved.

Listing of Prayers

Index of Authors/Sources

Notes

Notes

Notes